New Cities in America

THE LITTLE
RED BOOK
OF EVERYDAY HEROES

How Ordinary People
Can Become
Community Patriots

Sylvia L. Lovely

THE CLARK GROUP

LEXINGTON, KENTUCKY

DEDICATION

I would like to make a dedication once again to my parents, Walter and Alma Leach. My father at eighty-seven continues to amaze me with his wisdom; my mother, as she was dying, taught me how to live. I especially want to thank my dad for his stories, which I use liberally in my speeches and throughout this book, and my mother for allowing me to learn how important the stories of our past are to our future.

This book is also for our older son, Ross, his wife, Emma, and our younger son, David, for reminding me of how much hope we should have for the future. Today all three young people are active in their communities. Ross and David grew up "in the business" of civic engagement, watching mayors and civic leaders all their lives. I always hoped it would stick, and I think it did!

And finally I am dedicating the book to my husband, Bernie, for his inspiration and goodness. His calm demeanor and dedication to public service were especially valuable in his role as chairman of the airport board in Lexington, Ky., as it dealt with the tragic crash of Comair Flight 5191 that resulted in the deaths of 49 people in 2006.

ACKNOWLEDGMENTS

As I wrote my first book, *The Little Blue Book of Big Ideas,* John McGill was my helper/assistant/muse/editor and inspirer. His wonderful life came to an end when he died of cancer in March 2007 at age fifty-nine. John and I had grown so close, and our writing and thinking were so similar that I could start a sentence and he could finish it. In addition to being an incredibly talented and prolific writer, John was one of those special people we're lucky to know in life. He cared deeply about his community and the cause of civic engagement: Looking through his files after his death, it was clear that he had been thinking of a second book. We were able to use those thoughts and ideas in the preparation of this one.

Fifth Third Bank in Lexington and Louisville made this book possible with a generous grant. Fifth Third Bank's service to community is significant and longstanding. I have personally observed the countless hours of volunteer and community service by Phil McHugh, president of Fifth Third Bank in Louisville, and Sam Barnes, president of Fifth Third Bank in Lexington. I coined a phrase in *The Little Blue Book* describing people like Phil and Sam as community patriots. They and their employees surely deserve such a special designation.

Fran Ellers' long and distinguished career as a journalist and now writer and editor certainly prepared her to assist in the preparation of *The Little Red Book*. What is extraordinary beyond her way with words was her ability to step in and understand quickly and completely my goals with the book. In addition, Beverly Bartlett, another former journalist and also a novelist, conducted interviews and contributed in other important ways.

Of course this book would not have been possible without my colleagues at the Kentucky League of Cities and the NewCities Institute. NewCities was created by the board of the League to address issues of citizenship in the 21st century. I thank the boards of directors of those two organizations including Mayor David Willmoth, Jr. of Elizabethtown, president of the League and an exemplary elected official, and Virginia Fox, chair of the NewCities Institute, who built a national reputation as head of Kentucky Educational Television and went on to help set an education policy for the state. We are humbled that Virginia is so willing to share of her time and talents.

About the League and NewCities staff — what can I say? They are the most dedicated group of people with whom I have ever had the pleasure of working. The superb oversight of Neil Hackworth, a former mayor and KLC deputy executive director, gives our organization an edge.

ACKNOWLEDGMENTS

Bill Hamilton, KLC deputy director of insurance and finance services, goes above and beyond with his energy and creative thinking, and Tom Prather, executive vice president of NewCities, has breathed life and vigor into the organization in the two short years he has overseen its work. In addition, we could not do without the hard work of General Counsel Temple Juett and his legal staff.

The Little Red Book reflects the many contributions of Tad Long, NewCities director of business development, and NewCities consultant Steve Austin, whose work in Morehead, Ky., and Moscow, Idaho, was groundbreaking and important. Both cities are profiled in the following pages. And this book never would have made it to press without Bobbie Bryant, NewCities director of public affairs, who oversaw the project from beginning to completion. Bobbie never took her eye off the ball, calling me at all hours to remind me of deadlines and doing whatever it took to manage the work flow. Others who played key roles in the development of the book are Joseph Coleman, Ulysses Hayes, Doreen Caines, Terri Johnson, Robyn Miller, Kaye Smith and many others. As always I am obliged to Freda Meriwether, my executive assistant, who continues to inspire me with her own passion for community and making it better than she found it.

Finally, I want to recognize others who have inspired me to both write this book and dedicate my life to "telling the story" and showcasing those citizens who get up every morning and ask themselves, "How can I make this world a better place?" I thank Bobby Clark, CEO of The Clark Group, who has tirelessly "spread the word" about *The Little Red Book*; Steve Wrinn, director of the University of Kentucky Press, my good friend and inspirational leader who has generously given of his time and talents with expert advice not only to me but to my son David, whom he has chosen to mentor; and Dr. Doug Scutchfield, Bosomworth professor in the UK School of Public Health, who wakes up every morning with an agenda to make the world better.

I must also single out my friend Dr. James Ramsey, president of the University of Louisville, who was relentless in his pursuit of an important partnership with the NewCities Institute because of his belief that our youth are our future and we must find new and innovative ways to marry academic knowledge with Main Street needs. His friendship means more than he will ever know.

TABLE OF CONTENTS

FOREWORD

At Fifth Third Bank we are committed to building strong communities, and we believe that the money and resources we invest make an immediate and positive impact where we live and work.

As contributing members of the communities we serve, we see tremendous growth and vitality on the horizon, and we are dedicated to investing the time, resources and the people to help create the conditions for a better, stronger, more viable tomorrow.

Fifth Third Bank is proud to support the NewCitizen Kentucky partnership among the NewCities Institute, the Kentucky League of Cities, the Kentucky Community and Technical College System and other institutions of higher learning in Kentucky. It is our privilege to provide funding for *The Little Red Book of Everyday Heroes*, which will be presented to students who graduate from a community and technical college in Kentucky.

We are firm believers in excellence in education, and we know firsthand how important "everyday heroes" can be in the lives of students. Through Junior Achievement of the Bluegrass, volunteers from Fifth Third Bank and other local businesses share with students what it's like to run a company, work in the business world and be a smart consumer. Young people need these "everyday heroes" to help them make their way through school and through life. We support the Big Brothers/Big Sisters program in Lexington as well as other local educational initiatives, for the same reason.

Fifth Third Bank also understands how essential it is that citizens take responsibility for making our communities great. Fifth Third Bank employee volunteers in Louisville have helped refurbish the Americana Community Center, which provides support services to help families in the surrounding area — where 29 languages are spoken — assimilate into society and work toward successful futures. We also support the Society of St. Vincent de Paul, which provides assistance to homeless men, women and children to meet immediate needs and to help them become self-reliant and independent...creating a brighter future.

None of this would be possible without the support of our customers and community partners. Thank you for allowing us to serve your immediate and long-term financial needs and for working with us philanthropically to help build a better tomorrow.

FOREWORD

We look forward to all the good work and new ideas that will be garnered from *The Little Red Book of Everyday Heroes*.

Samuel G. Barnes,
President & CEO,
Fifth Third Bank
Central Kentucky

Philip R. McHugh,
President & CEO,
Fifth Third Bank Louisville

INTRODUCTION

When my colleagues and I at the NewCities Institute first came up with the concept for *The Little Red Book of Everyday Heroes*, we envisioned it as part of a trilogy of "little books" to explore a new definition of citizenship and community building for America's cities.

We wanted the books to be short enough to read on a plane or car trip, yet substantive enough to inspire civic leaders and ordinary citizens — the "community patriots" — whose contributions can make such a difference for their cities and communities. We decided on a patriotic theme: first a little blue book, then a little red book and last a little white book.

We believe it is imperative that cities and communities tap into the energy and ideas of their citizens because of the dramatic change they are experiencing in the age of technology. Some communities are growing at unprecedented speed while others are slowing down to retool. And all of them are reaching far beyond their borders — connecting, and often competing, on an international stage.

At the same time cities today must prepare for the catastrophic crises that could affect any community. I wrote *The Little Blue Book of Big Ideas* in the 9/11 era, when cities were focused on protecting themselves from overseas terrorists. Today we're in the era of Hurricane Katrina, an insane gunman at Virginia Tech and the bridge collapse in Minneapolis — when it's clear that some of the most serious threats to our communities may come from within.

At the NewCities Institute it is our belief that adapting to all this change — and change is the one constant for cities today — depends largely on citizens becoming more involved in local decision making. Many others, including economists, historians and government officials, have reached this same conclusion, citing the paradox of our modern "growing out of control" world. Theologian and scholar Larry Rasmussen put it this way: "The more 'planetary' our lives become, the more necessary small communities are."

This collaboration between elected officials and ordinary citizens is already happening in some communities, including several cities where NewCities has been a part of the process. Thus *The Little Red Book of Everyday Heroes* picks up where *The Little Blue Book of Big Ideas* left off. In this book, we explore the changes that cities and citizens are experiencing and introduce readers to some of the "everyday heroes," also known as community patriots, who are stepping up to lead their communities in the 21st century.

These everyday heroes are special people. They do not just engage in good works. They are true "citizens" who defy labels such as conservative and liberal, choosing instead to roll up their sleeves and make the world a better place one community at a time. Among other things, they have:

- a deep sense of caring for others and doing the right thing, which may put them at odds with their fellows and friends;
- a desire to encourage others and seek others' ideas;
- a certain conflict about decisions that are difficult but must be made; and
- a passion for results and for making a measurable difference.

Another goal of *The Little Red Book of Everyday Heroes* is to energize and inspire young people who, having studied the principles of civic engagement, are ready to get involved in their local communities.

To that end, the book will be a component of our NewCitizen Kentucky collaboration with Kentucky Community and Technical College System (KCTCS) and several of our state's institutions of higher education. NewCitizen Kentucky is intended to raise the civic capacity in Kentucky communities, creating new economic opportunities throughout the Commonwealth. The partnership will educate students — our future leaders — while providing safe harbors for city and county officials to collaborate, exchange ideas and resolve problems.

These institutions are leading the way in educating the community patriots who will be the key to their communities' progress in the 21st century. For instance:

- As a first step for NewCitizen Kentucky, President Michael McCall of the Kentucky Community and Technical College System, alongside the NewCities Institute, has instituted a year-long civic responsibility program for select community college students. In addition, KCTCS is redesigning its Phi Theta Kappa leadership course for honors students based on the NewCities 12 Principles of Community Building. It also supports programs to help community leaders adapt to change and opportunities for them to discuss complex issues.

- Commenting on community engagement, KCTCS President Michael McCall said, "If you've ever wondered how you could really help your community — and if it was worth the effort — you need to read *The Little Red Book of Everyday Heroes*. Sylvia Lovely and her NewCities Institute staff have gotten to the essence here: positive change begins with individual decisions, when people just like you and me make those first steps, big or small."

- To take NewCitizen Kentucky a step further, the University of Louisville will provide training in civic engagement for third- and fourth-year students through the Urban Solutions Center created by President Jim Ramsey and the NewCities Institute. The center will also be a resource for civic leaders and city administrators throughout Kentucky. In addition, U of L is home to the Citizenship Training Academy for students and is collaborating on a pilot project with the Kentucky Department of Education to develop civics courses for Kentucky high schools. It is also partnering with several other statewide officials and organizations, including Northern Kentucky University, on the Civic Literacy Initiative of Kentucky to enhance civic engagement throughout the state.

"My vision of encouraging civic involvement through programs on our campus has been realized through our relationship with the NewCities Institute and the Kentucky League of Cities," Dr. Ramsey said. "I'm proud that our students will have the opportunity to bring citizenship to life through real-world experiences as they further their education."

- Northern Kentucky University is deeply involved with local communities at the direction of President James Votruba, a leader of the region's Vision 2015 Initiative. President Votruba is also a national leader in the area of student civic engagement. The university houses the Scripps Howard Center for Civic Engagement and Nonprofit Development, the Outreach and Public Engagement project focusing on regional stewardship and the Library for Civic Engagement. NKU also supports the involvement of both faculty and students in community projects through several initiatives.

On education and civic engagement, Northern Kentucky University President Votruba remarked, "I have believed all of my professional life that the American university has more capacity to be a force for both individual and social progress than any other institution in the land. We harness this capacity through our research, teaching and dynamic civic engagement. Could there be more important work? Could there be more inspiring or renewing or poetic work? I don't think so!"

- Morehead State University's Institute for Regional Analysis and Public Policy has developed the NewCities Performance Scorecard and the NewCities Community Scorecard to help benchmark and track results of civic engagement initiatives over time. In addition, students in the Morehead State Leadership Development Program assume civic responsibility through projects on campus and in the community. Septemberfest, for example, celebrates democracy and the American community, and concludes with the presentation of awards for civic engagement initiatives among students and adults.

"The essence of our definition of regional engagement is that we take responsibility for passing on a better place to our children," said Morehead State President Wayne D. Andrews.

- The University of Kentucky offers both under-graduate and graduate degrees through its Department of Community and Leadership Development in the College of Agriculture. UK's Cooperative Extension Service provides educational programs in both leadership development and community economic development, and also conducts com-munity enhancement projects statewide. With ex-tension agents in all 120 of Kentucky's counties,

UK recognizes that sustainable rural development includes not only farmers but also the communities that provide the marketplace for their products. When citizens are engaged, farmers and city folk alike are the beneficiaries of the outcomes.

"We often hear people talk about the importance of leadership," said University of Kentucky President Lee T. Todd, Jr. "Leadership must start in our homes and our neighborhoods. We must become engaged in our community and work together with our friends, neighbors and colleagues to discover solutions to the complex issues that each of us face. When we do those things, we will all benefit from a stronger, livelier community."

- All of Kentucky's comprehensive state universities, including Morehead State, Northern Kentucky, Kentucky State, Murray State, Western Kentucky and Eastern Kentucky, are participating in the American Democracy Project, an initiative involving 225 campuses that help students understand and experience civic engagement. It is sponsored by the American Association of State Colleges and Universities and *The New York Times*.

These efforts add up to more than the sum of their parts. By prioritizing civic engagement both in the teaching of students and in community outreach, Kentucky's public colleges and universities are sending the message that it is a fundamental element of education. Many other higher education institutions across the country are doing the same thing, as are an increasing number of elementary and secondary schools.

And they're not doing it just because they "should." Not only is civic engagement critical to the future of our cities and communities in the 21st century, but it is a uniquely satisfying pursuit for all individuals. People want to contribute, to give back and to share what they can with their communities. It's just a matter of figuring out how.

We believe that by starting and building locally, citizens will prove us right. Strong local communities, knit together with each other, will create better regions, states, nations and, ultimately, a better world.

CHAPTER ONE

WHY WE ARE WRITING THIS BOOK

During a recent speaking engagement in Tucson, I was confronted by a young woman from another Arizona city who was clearly at her wit's end.

"I'm not leaving here," she declared, "until you tell me how to talk to my *stupid* mayor."

The moment was an epiphany of sorts for me. Here in the Internet age we can tap into our computers and become instant experts on virtually any topic. Yet we still do not understand – either as individual citizens or elected officials – how to engage each other in the messiness of democracy, especially under the new rules of the 21st century.

Certainly the pace of change has thrown many of our civic and elected officials for a loop, especially as traditional employers go by the wayside, technology takes over our work lives and young people move away to find the jobs or quality of life they're seeking.

Some city leaders — perhaps like the young woman's mayor, and certainly like the rest of us — are afraid of being swept away by forces they can't control. Still others work frantically to forestall problems or anticipate opportunities by adopting solutions that seem to have worked for other communities.

Yet more and more of them have realized that to ride this wave of change — and the next one, and the next one — they must tap the energy, ideas and commitment of their own citizens. And citizens are stepping up to the plate. Former Missoula, Mont., Mayor Daniel Kemmis put it this way in a recent issue of *The Kettering Review:*

"The one clearest, strongest and most democratic lesson that I learned from my tenure in the mayor's office was simply this: when it came to addressing the community's challenges and seizing its opportunities, Missoula was several thousand times smarter than I was ever going to be. It is that lesson that, more than anything else, continues to sustain my hope for democracy."

The NewCities Institute was founded to help citizens join with civic leaders to build great, sustainable communities where people come together to agree on a vision and make it a reality. Our 12 Principles of Community Building in the 21st century can be distilled into four P's: perspective, place, people and prosperity.

We piloted this work in two very different places: Moscow, Idaho and Morehead, Kentucky. What we found in both cities were citizens who were passionate about their communities and eager to share their thoughts and ideas. At the same time they wanted less talk and more action.

More importantly, as citizens and elected officials began collaborating, they began expecting more of each other. And each saw the other's participation as essential.

That said, engaging citizens is not quick or easy. In fact, it can be confusing, frustrating and time-consuming, as we also learned.

So why is it so essential?

Because, as we at NewCities like to say, the cavalry isn't coming — cities can no longer depend on a big auto plant riding into town with enough jobs to save the local economy or a federal windfall that will transform the storefronts on Main Street.

Nor can they necessarily depend on government alone when disaster strikes, a lesson that became all too clear during the tragic aftermath of Hurricane Katrina.

In fact, economic and political realities in the 21st century often depend on local initiatives:

- taking advantage, in a big or small way, of technological advances;
- making global connections, at a community level, with employers or customers;
- starting or developing small businesses; and
- improving the community's quality of life, including schools, health care and green space.

Yet even as we warn that there's no cavalry on the outskirts of town, we have good news, too: the cavalry's already here. Citizens are a city's greatest resource, both in envisioning its future and making that future a reality.

How do we know this? We've seen it in our own experience in Moscow and Morehead and observed it in other cities across America and the world.

But if cities are only as strong as their citizenry, we must do more to help citizens and community leaders engage with each other.

The young woman who asked for help with her mayor, for instance, wanted to turn an old hotel into transitional housing for the homeless. But she had no idea how to build support for her idea among elected officials and the public.

For their part, elected officials may not know what to do with an individual citizen's big idea or when and how to seek input from a broader cross-section of community residents.

Fortunately, we've learned that it's not an arduous task to teach citizens and communities about productive citizen engagement in the 21st century. Our first pilot program took a year; the second was completed in half that time. We've also discovered that much can be accomplished in only a month, or even a day.

Consider again the young woman from Tucson. That day several of us talked to her about gathering facts and building partnerships, and she quickly put it to use. Today, she is providing a vital community service for homeless residents – and says she has a new understanding of how to become involved in community life.

Perhaps the biggest challenge cities face, however, is coming to grips with what civic engagement really means today. We're used to thinking of it in traditional ways: citizens joining the Jaycees, for instance, or showing up to speak at a public meeting.

But because of social, cultural and economic forces, citizenship today is less about joining the PTA than about sharing individual skills and passions.

We're not just talking about "good works" and volunteerism; our communities need citizens to wrestle with the complexities of the community's most vexing issues. Take affordable housing for low income families, one of the biggest challenges for many communities. On average, 13 out of every 100 people in the U.S. live in poverty; so, in addition to building a single Habitat house in a particular community, why not look at changing housing policy altogether? In many ways it's a more difficult and time-consuming task. However, in the long run, it can do much more to make the community livable for people of all income levels.

"We need to look at front porches as crime-fighting tools, treat picnics as public health efforts and see choral groups as occasions of democracy," says Lew Feldstein of the New Hampshire Charitable Seminar and co-chair of the Saguaro Seminar: Civic Engagement in America, a project of *Bowling Alone* author Robert Putnam at the John F. Kennedy School of Government at Harvard.

Moreover, the citizens who may contribute the most social capital may not look like the "good citizens" we're used to. Leadership may come from anywhere.

I always chuckle when I think of the experience of one small Kentucky town several years ago. The town had depended for decades on an underwear plant that closed, eliminating more than 3,000 jobs. Soon, however, a major distributor moved from the West Coast into the cavernous space that had been abandoned, bringing with it employees who were relocating from California.

One day the mayor walked into a real estate office to see a young woman with purplish hair and multiple earrings in the waiting room. "She'll not get a home loan here," he predicted in the privacy of the real estate agent's office.

"She won't have to," came the reply. "She's the manager of the new plant. She can probably buy the bank."

The everyday heroes who can make a difference truly will come from all walks of life: they may be young or old, natives or transplants, traditional or nontraditional in their approach to life and work. Their contributions will come in many forms, from sharing their dreams for the community at a planning meeting to starting an art gallery in an abandoned building to running for office.

Engaging them is not only doable, it gets results. The NewCities prescriptive for citizens and elected leaders alike includes three basic steps:

- being informed about the community's strengths and opportunities;
- being inclusive so that citizens together with elected and civic leaders are setting priorities and examining options before a plan of action is proposed; and
- exerting leadership, including making bold decisions when consensus appears elusive.

This book will tell the stories of communities and citizens that are finding a way, on their own or with the help of NewCities, to ride the wave of change. It will include:

- a history of local community life in America and its significance in enhancing our appreciation for that ballyhooed but elusive quality called "citizenship";
- changes in the American lifestyle that have affected local community building;
- how those challenges can be turned into opportunities in America's communities — and why that matters; and
- how the bottom line comes down to people who are committed and enlightened — and why their stories must be told.

We will start by exploring why it can be so difficult for communities and citizens to change their ideas about what civic engagement and community building looks like. The answer lies in our history as communities and how it is changing dramatically in the 21st century.

CHAPTER TWO

HOW CITIES HAVE CHANGED OVER TIME

I have years of formal education beyond his eight, but my 87-year-old dad always manages to get the best of me.

Being the Depression-era bargain hunter that he is, we were looking through the grocery ads during my weekly visit with him. I announced proudly that I had recently gone to an organic food store to buy free-range chicken for dinner. "It may cost more, but it's better for you," I said. "These chickens peck around the barn floor just like the chickens when you were young!"

He paused a moment and looked at me. "I've seen those 'natural' chickens and what they eat," he said. "I'll stick to getting my chicken at Wal-Mart." Zinged again!

Don't pine for the good old days — he was wisely reminding me — when you don't really know what they were like. That can be especially tempting as we talk about community building and citizenship. At times it seems we've lost so much compared to the way things used to be. Weren't our neighbors more caring, our communities more close-knit, our problems more manageable a few decades ago?

And then the question becomes: How do we find our way now? Our world is changing faster than we can absorb it. No sooner had we gotten used to the idea of the "information age" than we were told to watch out for the "conceptual age," the phrase coined by author Daniel Pink. And no sooner did we recognize that citizens are increasingly alienated by politics than we are told we must "engage" them for the sake of our future.

To say the least, it's hard to keep up.

It's to be expected that we would superimpose outdated assumptions onto updated realities. We imagine, for instance, if we could get more people into churches or civic groups, we'd have more citizen involvement in public life. Or perhaps if we did a better job of marketing our city's "comprehensive plan," the public would support it.

What's missing in both examples is the essence of civic engagement today: bringing citizens together with elected leaders before deciding "what's best," both for the community and their own roles in civic life. If this isn't done earlier, it will be all but impossible to muster their support for some of the changes today's cities must contemplate to sustain themselves.

Here's a look at how we have come to view cities and citizenship as we do and how the reality is changing.

The purpose of cities

What exactly is a city? In many ways the word "city," a derivative of the ancient word *civitas* or "citizen," is more a verb than a noun. A city links its citizens to a vast array of services and opportunities that they otherwise would not have. It links people to each other, fostering a strong sense of community and concern.

A city thrives when its citizens collaborate to improve living conditions. At its best, a city is a collective idea, an unspoken agreement by its citizens to stand side by side through life's hardships and celebrations. At its best, it is home.

Said playwright and poet William Shakespeare:

"What is the city but the people?"

It is no accident that many historians describe the first forming of cities as the beginning of civilized man. Without cities, the civilization that has been laboriously built over the past millennia could never have happened.

Cities began for a variety of reasons. The first ones were small, primitive communities where citizens lived, worked and played together in order to have more opportunities for economic success. Citizens were able to share abilities and talents to produce more and trade with one another. These communities continued to develop and, over time, became more densely populated.

Also over time, they began taking on different functions. Cities began serving as centers of religion, defense, government, trade and commerce. Dominant in scholarship and housing great universities, laboratories and libraries and art galleries, cities became the cultural centers as well.

That is still the case today, though the function of cities is still evolving. One reason is ever-changing ideas about what it means to come together to do in concert what cannot be done alone. Thus modern era local governments were formed in the United States when the population increased beyond the size that could be accommodated by New England-style town meetings.

Still, today's city governments provide for the needs of their residents: safety to walk the streets, roads to get to the grocery or to work, parks for leisure pursuits. Additionally, they provide for clean water, waste disposal and utility services.

They also tend to take on responsibility for "community building," or enhancing the city's economic, cultural and social attributes. But at the end of the day there's only so much its leaders can do.

In reality, as Shakespeare suggested, a city's potential is influenced most by its citizens.

A refresher on the history of cities and communities in the U.S.

Back when George Washington was running the country, only five percent of people lived in cities, and small cities at that. Everyone else lived in rural America according to the 1790 census. They stayed close to home given the limits of transportation: walking, riding a horse, hitching the horse to a wagon or going by boat.

In the few "big" cities, the wealthiest residents lived close to downtown near businesses and amenities. The middle class lived a little further out, and the poor even further.

Things began changing over the next 50 years. The number and size of cities grew as a result of industrialization: steamboats, the cotton gin, grain elevators, etc. Railroads accelerated industrialization in the middle 1800s. River cities boomed by adding busy factories to their downtowns where rail and river traffic could intersect.

And starting in 1842 Americans looking for adventure or a better life began heading west on the Oregon Trail, thus creating more small communities that eventually grew into cities.

Moving to the outskirts

By the late 1800s cities were becoming crowded and less livable given unsanitary conditions and the smoke from factories and businesses. In time, streetcars and commuter rail lines made it possible for wealthier families to add a second home in the country or to move permanently to the city's edge.

Eventually the growing middle class gravitated to homes further outside the city's center. Poor families who didn't have access to carriages or money for a streetcar ride continued to live in the less desirable parts of downtown.

City centers were changing too. They were more segmented with retail, industrial and local government areas. The development of skyscrapers in the late 1800s allowed metropolitan cities to concentrate office space for white-collar workers. City leaders also began dealing with a range of growing pains from crime to political corruption.

But cities were still the place to be. By 1870 more than one-third of Americans lived in cities. By 1920 more than half did. Put another way, 10 million Americans lived in cities in 1870 and 54 million by 1920.

Even where cities didn't spring up, smaller communities did, especially in rural areas like the Appalachian region where I was born. Recently an aunt sent me an old magazine with the headline "Mize's 'First Nine' — Morgan

County Baseball Team — 1914." Typical of the era, none of the nine young men in the accompanying photograph was smiling — save one. My grandfather, 28 at the time, was sporting a mischievous grin. In that era in rural America it didn't get much better than being one of the hometown players of the national pastime on a field of green.

The article noted how every little town across Kentucky had a baseball team. That no doubt held true throughout the American heartland. Those motley teams, likely consisting of young farmers and few men holding "day" jobs, traveled from small town to small town rarely if ever venturing beyond a circle larger than 30 to 50 miles. The towns had names like Mize or Hazel Green or Grassy Creek, and there was a "big" city at the center. How exciting it must have been for my grandfather to go to West Liberty, the Morgan County seat.

But already society was changing in ways that would affect those tiny communities forever. By 1920 the automobile had become affordable and popular. Families were more mobile and continued to move to larger cities. It wasn't long before Mize, Ky., my grandfather's hometown, was little more than a sign on the highway.

Of course they were not as free to "move up" during the Depression years of the 1930s and World War II in the 1940s, but many moved on. Desperate economic conditions led some rural families — especially those in Appalachia, where opportunities were even more scarce — to seek out factory jobs in what was their promised land, the industrialized northern United States. My parents were among them, leaving rural Kentucky for steady factory work for my father in Dayton, Ohio.

Suburbia

After World War II, the GI bill helped veterans pay for college and obtain home loans. Cars were essential by now, and freeways made it easier to commute to work. Young couples began buying inexpensive homes in the suburbs outside the city limits in hastily developed neighborhoods of similar-style houses. The most famous was the much-lampooned suburb of Levittown, N.Y., where developers in the late 1940s and early 1950s produced thousands of inexpensive small homes to rent or buy.

Air conditioning meant front porches were no longer necessary; families began socializing in the private confines of the backyard. All those surburban houses soon had televisions, which kept families at home in the evenings rather than with friends and neighbors. Businesses and retail establishments began moving to the suburbs to be closer to workers and shoppers.

The Interstate Highway System created in 1956 changed the national landscape even more dramatically. Business and industry began locating along highway exits, and families gained the freedom to travel by car throughout the country. City centers were left to deal with urban decay and a changing tax base.

By the 1980s the downtowns of even small cities began to look abandoned, especially as "big box" discount stores such as Wal-Mart outside the city limits began competing with downtown retailers. My father put it this way: "People used to go to town to trade. Now they go out of town!"

Shifting economics

City and suburb dwellers were still depending on jobs at factories and manufacturing plants, but that too was changing. Between 1970 and 2000, the service industry (insurance, banking, retail, education, government, tourism) increased employment by more than 200 percent and overtook manufacturing as the largest slice of the economic pie. Manufacturing dropped from 22 percent of the economy in 1970 to 11.5 percent in 2000; the service industry increased from 19 to 32 percent in the same time period according to the Brookings Institution.

The economy changed again — and much more dramatically — when the so-called "information age" swept the country starting in the 1980s. Because of technological advances, businesses and industry began rapidly incorporating computers into their workplaces. Families, schools and governments followed soon after. According to the 2000 Census more than half of the country's homes had at least one computer.

As a result, the manufacturing and service sectors of the economy have now been overtaken in some ways by the "creative" sector, according to Richard Florida's book *Cities and the Creative Class*, which follows on his much-quoted *The Rise of the Creative Class*.

Florida cites research that shows that more than half of all income from wages and salaries in the U.S. is earned by creative workers in the fields of science and technology; arts, culture and design; and the "knowledge-based professions" of health care, finance and the law. That's more than the manufacturing and service sectors combined.

Today's cities

According to the Brookings Institution's analysis of urban life in 2006 America is going through dramatic, volatile change "comparable in scale and complexity to the latter part of the 19th century."

Not only are there similarities to industrialization in the impact of the technological revolution, but the U.S. is again growing at an unprecedented pace in large part because of immigration from Latin America, Asia and Africa.

Every state experienced population growth in the 1990s for the first time in the 20th century, according to Brookings. The U.S. grew by 33 million people in that decade, which was the size of the entire country on the eve of the Civil War (by comparison, the population grew by 22 million in the 1980s and 23 million in the 1970s).

The makeup of households is also changing. The nuclear family of married parents with kids in school makes up fewer than one-quarter of households. One-fourth of us are living alone, and others are living together unmarried or living with other family members or friends. We're also, as we've heard many times, getting older.

Community life has come nearly full circle since Washington's day. Then, nine out of 10 of us lived in the country. Today, three out of four of us are living in the city. One report from the University of Pennsylvania suggests that within 40 years most of the U.S. population will live in or around eight "super cities" on the coasts and in Florida, Texas and parts of the Midwest and South.

That doesn't mean that small towns in rural America have gone by the wayside. Because people can live and work anywhere, the success of each town is more dependent than ever on local determination. There are 19,429 cities and towns in America according to the National League of Cities. Nearly half of them have fewer than 1,000 residents while 58 have 300,000 or more, including the largest, New York City.

Some are sprawling growth centers on the coasts; others are mere shadows of previously dynamic economic centers of yesteryear. Some — like Chicago and Minneapolis — have thriving and beautifully restored downtowns; others like Los Angeles and Houston — are spread out with no discernable center.

But virtually all of them are struggling to decide how they'll sustain themselves through the 21st century.

CHAPTER THREE

WHAT IT TAKES TO BUILD A CITY TODAY: THE FOUR P'S

So how *will* cities and communities sustain themselves? The NewCities Institute has learned in our work over the last several years that thriving cities have several characteristics in common. We described them as the 12 Principles of Community Building in *The Little Blue Book of Big Ideas*.

For our purposes here, we will break them down into what we call the Four P's: perspective, place, people and prosperity.

Gaining perspective

"A city needs to see itself as it really is, as well as to see a glorious vision of itself in the eye of faith."

E. L. Thorndike, *Your City*

Where does your city fit in the global community?

The world is flat, *The New York Times* columnist Thomas Friedman tells us, and surely it's becoming clearer every day that technology has all but eliminated geographical borders in our economic and work lives.

While this opens up tremendous opportunities to sell our goods or services overseas, it also poses a threat. We're no longer just competing with a city an hour away for, say, a regional distribution center. We're competing with cities around the globe for talent and jobs.

Certainly the "think globally, act locally" catch-phrase doesn't go far enough any more. We must think globally and locally at the same time as well as take action in our own backyards and on other continents.

Obviously, gaining this perspective takes work. Some of the work involves becoming better informed about the world around us. Some of it involves becoming better informed about our own communities.

You've heard the old saying that the only fish that understands water is a flying fish. When we're immersed in an environment, it's hard to see ourselves or our cities objectively.

Yet the view from 30,000 feet is critical. What strengths and possibilities in our community might we be looking at but not seeing? And how might we connect with other communities, states, countries or continents to build on them?

Sometimes cities gain this perspective the hard way. In the early 1990s United Airlines decided to locate a maintenance center in Indianapolis rather than Oklahoma City in part because United employees said they didn't want to live in Oklahoma City as there wasn't much to do.

Oklahoma City's citizens took note — and took action. They approved a one-cent sales tax over five years to raise money for a revitalization effort that included a new convention center, a sports center, a renovated music hall and an entertainment and dining district downtown. The efforts paid off; aerospace and technology companies have since moved to Oklahoma City.

It can be thrilling to realize how much we can share in a flat world, not just by using technology, but by talking to each other. At a recent National League of Cities seminar I found myself sitting beside Abdel Menhem Aris, the mayor of Beirut, Lebanon. In my usual way of introducing myself to people whom I assume could not possibly know about my state, I said, "I'm from Kentucky — you know, the Derby, Kentucky Fried Chicken."

He quickly replied, "My dear, I have lived in Louisville, Paducah ... and Central City," a small town nearby.

And with that, the world seemed to shrink a bit more.

NewCities Principles: Perspective
Adapt to change by being informed
Connect to the outside world
Start locally, go globally

Paying attention to place

"The enduring competitive advantages in a global economy lie increasingly in local things - knowledge, relationships and motivation that distant rivals cannot match."

Michael Porter, Harvard Business School and
Harvard's Institute for Strategy and Competitiveness

Back in the late 1980s and early 1990s, the newspaper in Louisville, Ky., began profiling cities throughout Kentucky in a weekly feature called "Our Towns."

The idea was to describe the distinguishing characteristics of Kentucky's many small communities. Yet time and again reporters found the same old story: a Wal-Mart on the edge of town had perhaps dealt the final blow to the retail district downtown. Some cities were still growing, but that growth was typically measured in the number of chain restaurants and home stores that had sprung up on the city outskirts near a parkway or interstate.

In truth, small-town residents often saw the proliferation of chains as a benefit of sorts. They might say, "Yes, we have the same amenities as the big cities! Wal-Mart and Home Deport and Costco chose *us*!"

By the same token, if one community can't be distinguished from another one down the road, why would an employer or young family or retired couple choose to move there? Indeed, cities and suburbs may be able to survive for awhile on fast-foot chains, but they can't sustain themselves for long on such fare. They must focus instead on what they uniquely have to offer. The alternative is to become dependent on the fortunes of mega-corporations located somewhere else.

Close your eyes for a moment and think: Why do you choose to live where you do? What's different about your city than another city you might choose?

You may be thinking in terms of your city's geography, history, local culture or workforce skills. Taken together, they add up to a sense of "place" that reflects the quality of life citizens enjoy.

Giant benefits firm Mercer Human Resource Consulting every year ranks cities by "quality of life," which is of concern to companies that may be asking employees to relocate to another city around the globe. The leading American cities tend to be those with distinct identities such as Honolulu, San Francisco and Boston.

Conversely, some kinds of companies pay attention to place by congregating in communities where they believe they can attract creative, talented employees, according to Richard Florida in *The Rise of the Creative Class*. Think Silicon Valley, the San Francisco Bay Area, Seattle.

Agreeing on that "sense of place," on who we are, is critically important for local communities. One of my favorite stories resulting from the Hurricane Katrina disaster was of the attempt to turn Biloxi, Miss., into a hotbed of new urbanism. It was nice to think about morphing into a city of quaint yet gentrified homes, neighborhoods and stores.

But that just wasn't Biloxi. The plan was rejected by the city's residents who felt strongly that wanted to remain true to their culture as the last great coastal working-class town in America.

NewCities Principles: Place
Play to strengths and uniqueness
Plan and develop over time
Steward the environment

Investing in people

"What keeps downtowns alive is not money but people who care."

Paul Felt, managing editor, *Downtown Idea Exchange*

Some communities despair when they realize that the "knowledge economy" is different from what has sustained them in the past: manufacturing plants or farm land or coal, for example.

Yet today's new "natural resource" is people — not just people who can fill workforce needs, but people who can start companies, contribute to the tax base and help a community improve its quality of life.

This isn't such a new concept. The noted city historian Lewis Mumford made the case for investing in people in *The City in History* in 1961. Florida explored why this is getting even more attention today in *The Rise of the Creative Class*. Economic growth depends today on the three T's, he says: technology, talent and tolerance. All three depend on human capital.

And yet focusing on people goes beyond advising cities to try to attract tech-savvy industries and their highly skilled workers. It means investing in local education programs in order to "grow our own" creative minds.

It also means more than tolerating the usual differences of sexual orientation or ethnicity in order to provide a little diversity. It involves actively including and encouraging people of all different cultures, backgrounds and walks of life.

This, of course, is easier said than done. Recently Lexington, Ky., where I live, launched an initiative called "Erasing Racism." Some rightly argue that Lexington is coming late to this idea. Yet it takes a certain amount of courage for a community to publicly pinpoint and address racial discrimination 40 years after the civil rights movement.

At the same time, of course, we cannot erase the tragic history of slavery with a single initiative. But what we can do, and what Lexington is doing, is to implement a process for ongoing conversation that I hope will never end. The discussions so far have led to people-oriented projects such as Get On Board, sponsored by the local United Way, to increase the number of African-Americans and other minorities who serve on the boards of organizations that make things happen in Lexington.

But the key for the community is to keep talking, even and perhaps especially when the subject is so difficult. While the United Way effort is an "excellent example of what can happen when a community makes a serious effort to change," says local Urban League President and CEO P.G. Peeples, "real change will be tied to creating more economic opportunities for minorities. That is the part of the conversation that has not been prominent in the past but certainly needs to be on the table more often."

There are other kinds of inclusiveness as well. I know a young college graduate who recently found a job he really liked installing heating and air conditioning systems in new buildings. He was concerned, however, about "lowering" his sights after completing his higher education.

Certainly he doesn't fit the stereotype of the hip young Ivy League graduate whom so many communities try to attract.

But what a narrow, damaging stereotype that is of the ideal citizen of the future — unfair to the Ivy Leaguers and everyone else! We should cater to and validate my young friend's ambition as much as anyone else's, and not just because it's the right thing to do. People who pursue what they like and love are the people who can help a community pursue a vision.

At the same time we can't forget the people who don't have so many options — the young people who drop out of school, and those who aren't included in the leadership programs that are filled with pleasant and well-situated young professionals. Unless our communities can help them find a foothold, we'll lose ground again.

Thus while many schools and communities are focused on encouraging STEM — science, technology, engineering and math – our goal can't only be to turn out professionals in lab coats and Ph.D. scientists. Improving math skills will help in a number of areas that improve lives on a daily basis — from increasing financial literacy to running the local water company.

Instead of concentrating only on attracting the creative class, then, perhaps we should be trying harder to create places where people of all types — whether society considers them extraordinary or ordinary — will be able to thrive.

NewCities Principles: People
Foster leadership
Be inclusive
Meet people's basic needs (education, arts, health)

Building prosperity

"If you want one year of prosperity, grow grain. If you want 10 years of prosperity, grow trees. If you want 100 years of prosperity, grow people."

Attributed to everyone from Francis Bacon to
Adlai Stevenson to a Chinese proverb

While lecturing on building economic prosperity in the 21st century, a speaker recently noted that it's no longer about "trickle down" or "trickle up" economics. It's about "trickle all around" — the globe, that is.

Thus it is about doing all things all the time: recruiting big businesses and incubating small ones, supporting existing employers while staking entrepreneurs.

It's also about redefining our notion of "economic development." Today, sustainable communities are the ones building on their strengths, defying the naysayers. And in the process, they're inspiring the rest of us.

What communities must do is play to their strengths while creating a climate for change and innovation, for that help their residents build wealth, and wealth is partly defined by quality of life.

City economists say that none of us can predict what business models will be successful in years to come. It was once conventional wisdom, for instance, that we would all purchase everything over the Internet and love it. That didn't pan out. Companies such as Dell have learned that people still desire human contact, thus Dell is now opening retail stores.

In the same way, we could not have predicted gas prices, the conservation movement or the popularity of certain cars 10 years ago.

Yet, we often as communities, figure we should look for emerging trends — or what has worked for a neighboring city — and try that. Certainly trends can trigger good ideas about how to play to our strengths and seize opportunities. But because they are ever-changing, we can't depend on either the good news or the bad to justify our community-building strategies.

Consider Florence, Ariz., home to an assortment of private and state-run maximum security prisons. The civic leaders of yesteryear were given the choice of building a state university or a state prison. They chose the prison because of the need for immediate jobs for the townspeople.

Today we might wonder at such a choice and whether the community regrets it. Yet Florence residents feel safe and happy, and the town is still growing. Its leaders and citizens making adjustments when the time comes.

The magazine *Fast Company* annually identifies a list of "Fast Cities" from Shanghai to Boise, Idaho, which are experiencing growth and attracting people. How do they do it?

According to the magazine in 2007, "It starts with opportunity. Not just bald economic capacity, but a culture that nurtures creative action and game-changing enterprise." The second element is innovation, and the third is energy, "that ethereal thing that happens when creative people collect in one place."

In truth, many communities have these elements without realizing it. Whether they can benefit, however, depends on their self-esteem — yes, cities have self-esteem issues too! The most successful are the ones who esteem themselves enough to say, "We will, we can, we are *determined* to do so."

In the movie *Apollo 13*, for instance, the crippled spacecraft is stuck somewhere near the moon and the astronauts must get it back.

Back on Earth, the spacecraft engineers — pocket protectors and all — are in the mission control building in Houston. One of them dumps on the table all the items available on the space ship. "Gentleman," he says, "this is what they have up there, and this is what *you* have to get that space ship back from the moon."

They set to work and the result was…well, obviously the ending was a good one. The point is this: If local communities take what they have at hand and "see the possible," they can get things moving again.

NewCities Principles: Prosperity
Recruit, retain and generate wealth
Think big and small at the same time
Rethink boundaries

To address the Four P's, cities must begin to think differently about how citizens can contribute to community building. That means understanding how the circumstances of citizens' lives are changing in the 21st century — and how to make the most of it.

CHAPTER FOUR

AS CITIES CHANGE, SO DOES COMMUNITY LIFE

If all the change that has been discussed thus far can be summed up quickly, it would be that (1) each of us is more mobile and lack a certain kind of rootedness to place, (2) we are exposed to more and more information of a worldwide nature and (3) the definition of self and one's relationship to others in community has become confused, sometimes resulting in citizen apathy and a feeling of helplessness in the face of a vast universe.

So, what is the impact of each on our community life?

Mobility

The best stories are often those that are not intended for your own ears. Not long ago I overheard a conversation involving Rekha, who had migrated with her family first from India to New York City, where she was educated.

Rekha had begun her career as a journalist at *The Des Moines Register* in Iowa, where both she and her husband worked. She was a "fish out of water," she observed. Soon, the couple sought and found jobs in South Florida at a large newspaper.

But much to their surprise, they both immediately missed Iowa. They applied for and got back their old jobs. "I guess I missed being around real people and having farmers argue with me about my columns," Rekha said.

Rekha's experience does not differ from that of many people today. We may live, work or go to school in many different places, but ultimately we all yearn for some quality of life that can be identified with a particular place. And, it seems, we increasingly yearn for authenticity.

That we have much greater choice in where that place will be is one of the benefits of the technological age. If we want to live in rural America, we may be able to telecommute for a major employer in a big city. We also have a window to the world in the Internet. From our home computers, we can explore places and possibilities we might never have considered before.

Coming and going

Yet all this moving around means that most communities must continually adjust to gaining or losing people — and, at times, their employers, who contribute more than just jobs to the community. Many cities, for instance, depend on corporate contributions to the arts or social services. However, today's corporations are increasingly dividing their "home offices" among several cities or states, which also spreads their corporate largesse among more locations.

More important is the effect of mobility on social capital, or the wealth that is created by connections among citizens and local leaders. In fast-growing communities an infusion of new people can be energizing, helping us think "out of the box" about the possibilities for our future. It can also be disconcerting as we struggle to connect with people whom we don't know, who have different cultural norms and who may not be as invested in the community as we are.

Or perhaps they're just not invested in the same things.

Sandie Smith, a county commissioner in Pinal County, Ariz., told me about one such conflict in her growing community. Local citizens prize the wide-open skies so much that they limit street lighting so they can see the stars at night. But a couple who recently moved to Pinal County from Phoenix, attracted by "more house" for the money, complained to Sandie about — you guessed it — the lack of street lights.

It would have been easy to roll one's eyes at the newcomers' complaint. But Sandie, a great public servant, was genuinely interested in their quandary of parents wanting to walk at night with their young children and not in the dark. To her, changing faces in the community meant the community itself was changing. Thus it would be important to bring the couple into Pinal County's conversation about how to meet the needs of everyone who wants to enjoy the night sky.

Immigration

And yet what if that infusion of people changes the ethnic and cultural makeup of a community, virtually overnight?

Families from Latin America, Asia and Africa are now a growing part of many communities. Immigration, of course, is hardly new to America. Our earliest settlers were immigrants who came in wave after wave, settling in a Little Ireland here and a Little Italy there and Chinatowns galore. There is a natural tendency, after all, to settle close to those who look like you, talk like you and come from the same culture.

The difference today is in how this immigrant population is dispersed. Rather than settling for the most part in larger cities, immigrants now go to all parts of the country to work everything from horse farms to fast food restaurants.

Again, it would be easy for communities to become overwhelmed as they try to meet the needs of these new citizens, especially those who are just learning English. The challenges for public schools alone can be daunting.

Yet successful communities are focusing on the opportunities offered by cultural diversity as much as the challenges and integrating cultural lessons into everyday life. I saw that approach first-hand recently while visiting Arthur Byrn, the mayor of Mayfield, Ky., a city with a population around 10,300. Arthur reported to me that a number of

Mexican restaurants had opened up in his city, and he offered to treat me to lunch at one of his favorites.

When we entered the restaurant a young man came over immediately and began talking to Arthur in Spanish. To my surprise the mayor replied haltingly in Spanish as well. Once we were seated, the young man again spoke in Spanish as he went over the specials of the day. And Arthur again responded in Spanish, however tentatively.

"What was that all about?" I asked after they'd finished.

Arthur said that he and his family visited the restaurant often, and the young man had taken it upon himself to ask the mayor if he would like to learn Spanish. Arthur took him up on it.

What might seem like a small moment between the mayor and the young man isn't so small after all. It shows how community life can be enhanced as we learn to appreciate each other's backgrounds and talents. It all begins at the local level.

Losing population

Of course a community's priorities may also change when people are leaving rather than arriving. Low- or no-growth communities may be drained of energy when they lose population, either because jobs are no longer available or people are seeking a different kind of life. It can be a fearful time for those who remain. Will their city continue to wither and eventually die? What will happen to their jobs, their lifestyles, the value of their homes and possessions?

Yet some cities have found a way to make lemonade out of this predicament — take Youngstown, Ohio. A former boom town for the steel industry, Youngstown has embraced a strategy of "shrinking" after factory closures left the community a shadow of its former self. The idea is to replace abandoned property with green space and make other changes to improve the quality of life and strengthen the smaller community that now exists. Youngstown, in other words, has reinvented itself as a "small town."

Other cities are drawing on these lessons, including Richmond, Va., St. Louis, Mo., and Detroit, Mich. Not every community can sustain itself during such a dramatic economic downturn, but these stories tell us something more: cities that are flexible in the face of change will find ways to make change work for them.

Information overload

In the early days of 24-hour TV news during the Gulf War I was a big fan. "All-day news!" I exulted. It had to be so much better than silly sitcoms and mindless talk shows!

In the Beginning….

The NewCities Institute convened "The Morphing of Main Street, USA" at Centre College in Danville, Ky., in September 2001. This event created the NewCities Institute 12 Principles of Community Building.

Working together at "The Morphing of Main Street, USA" in September 2001 to create the NewCities Institute 12 Principles of Community Building were: (L - R) The Courier-Journal Columnist Betty Baye, NewCities President Sylvia L. Lovely, former Secretary of Housing and Urban Development Henry Cisneros, NewCities Board Chairman Virginia G. Fox and former Kentucky Secretary of the Executive Cabinet Crit Luallen.

In September 2001 experts in community development gathered from around the country to discuss our changing world; the result of their work was the development of the NewCities Institute 12 Principles of Community Building.

NewCity Moscow, Idaho
America's First NewCity

A large crowd gathers for the NewCity Moscow kick-off celebration.

Judy Brown, an everyday hero in Moscow, Idaho.

L – R: NewCities Institute Executive Vice President Tom Prather and President Sylvia L. Lovely discuss NewCity Moscow with University of Idaho President Timothy White.

NewCity Moscow, Idaho

*Moscow City Council: (L – R) John Weber, Linda Pall,
Aaron Ament, Nancy Chaney (Mayor), Bill Lambert,
the late John Dickinson and Bob Stout.*

*Moscow Mayor
Nancy Chaney.*

*(Photo Courtesy of
Archer Photography,
Johnathan S. Billing,
Moscow, Idaho).*

*Citizens of Moscow, Idaho, discuss possibilities for
their community at the NewCity Moscow charrette.*

NewCity Moscow, Idaho

Residents of Moscow, Idaho, visit the Farmers Market to learn about NewCity Moscow from NewCities Institute staff Tad Long and Steve Austin.

A bird's-eye view of Moscow, Idaho.

Moscow Councilmember Linda Pall.

(Photo Courtesy of Archer Photography: Johnathan S. Billing, Moscow, Idaho).

NewCity Morehead, Kentucky
Kentucky's First NewCity

Morehead State University President Wayne D. Andrews and NewCities Institute President Sylvia L. Lovely enjoy the NewCities Morehead kick-off event.

Dudley Herron, an exemplary community patriot in Morehead.

Brian Gay and friends at the Campus Cookout event for his fraternity. (L – R) Frank Hatten, Rebekah Jackson, Brian Gay, Kris King and Steven Potter. (Photo Courtesy of Brian G. Gay).

NewCity Morehead, Kentucky

Kick-off event for NewCity Morehead, Ky.

U.S. Congressman Hal Rogers, representing Kentucky's Fifth District, along with William Roach-Barrette, a 5th-grade student at Botts Elementary School in Morehead, Ky. William led the NewCity Morehead kick-off event with the Pledge of Allegiance.

Morehead Mayor Bradley Collins with his granddaughter, Danielle Staton.

Sparks, Nevada Leadership Summit

Sparks, Nev., continues to grow and expand.

Linda Patterson is the executive administrator for the city manager in Sparks. She serves her community as a public employee and shows how to become everyday heroes in our own hometowns.

"Making lemonade out of lemons:" Sparks transformed a gravel pit into a beautiful downtown lake and marina.

Romania
Seeking the Possible Through Citizen Engagement

Romanian Palace of the Parliament in Bucharest. The Romanian Chamber of Deputies and the Senate conduct state business in the Palace. Originally built by Communist President Nicolae Ceauşescu, it is the second largest public building in the world—only exceeded by the U.S. Pentagon. Ceauşescu forced 20,000 Romanians who worked 24/7, 365 days a year for six years to build this monument to himself. He was deposed and executed in the Revolution of 1989 without ever seeing its completion. The building is constructed entirely of Romanian materials.

Gheorghe Bunduc, president of the Tulcea County Council, hosted a banquet for the NewCities team at a lakeside retreat. He invited traditional Romanian dancers to perform especially for his guests – and perform they did!

Romania

Minister Marin Cojoc and his staff meet with the NewCities team in Bucharest. Minister Cojoc is the Director General Adjunct of the Ministry of Public Finance.

Sirma Caraman, president of the Association of Financial Managers from Romanian Public Administration, hosted the NewCities Institute team in 2007 to establish a partnership between the two organizations. Mrs. Caraman (left) and Sylvia Lovely are pictured here in the gardens of a Bucharest park.

Romania

During a river cruise through the Danube Delta in Tulcea, board members of the Association of Financial Managers from Romanian Local Public Administration discuss issues related to citizen engagement and transparency in governance with NewCities executive staff.

Mayor Ionel Charita and his family welcome Sylvia Lovely and other members of the NewCities team to their home. Monica Mindru, executive director of the Association of Financial Managers from Romanian Local Public Administration and former visiting scholar with the NewCities Institute, is standing to the left of Mayor Charita.

Senator Aurel Gabriel Simionescu, member of the Romanian Parliament from Tulcea County and NewCities President Sylvia Lovely exchanged gifts during their meeting on the Danube Delta.

NewCitizen Kentucky

Dr. Michael B. McCall, Kentucky Community and Technical College System president, and Sylvia L. Lovely, Kentucky League of Cities executive director/ CEO and NewCities Institute president, celebrate NewCitizen Kentucky, a new partnership among the three organizations.

A real community hero, P.G. Peeples, Urban League president and CEO, Lexington, Ky.

Enthusiastic supporters of NewCities Institute: (L - R) Kentucky League of Cities Deputy Executive Director Neil S. Hackworth and Deputy Director of Insurance and Finance Services Bill Hamilton with Bill Nighbert, former KLC president and mayor of Williamsburg, Ky.

Urban Solutions Center
Louisville, Kentucky

NewCities Institute Executive Vice President Tom Prather shares information about the Urban Solutions Center at the University of Louisville, Louisville, Ky.

2007 Kentucky League of Cities President and Elizabethtown Mayor David L. Willmoth, Jr., with Lexington Ky. Mayor Jim Newberry and KLC staff member Anthony Wright during the Mayors' Luncheon in Louisville, Ky., where the Urban Solutions Center at the University of Louisville was unveiled.

Urban Solutions Center
Louisville, Kentucky

*Dedicated community patriots, Nashville Tenn. Mayor Bill Purcell
and Louisville Ky. Mayor Jerry Abramson.*

*A true community patriot,
Dr. James Ramsey,
president of the University
of Louisville, our partner
with the Urban Solutions
Center.*

NewCity
Madisonville-Hopkins County
A Citizen Driven Process to Chart the Community's Future

Residents draw and discuss their dreams during the NewCity Madisonville-Hopkins County, Ky. charrette.

Madisonville Mayor Will Cox, Jr., shares ideas from his team at the charrette in Madisonville, Ky.

Tables of citizens get into the action of designing their community at the NewCity Madisonville-Hopkins County charrette.

Flagstaff, Arizona
Citizens Involved . . . Making a Difference

Lynette and Kent Bybee take a moment to relax at the Royal Inn, a transitional housing business in Flagstaff, Ariz.

Visitors at the Royal Inn in Flagstaff, Ariz., celebrate the holidays with a community meal.

A very special thanks to our sponsor

Samuel G. Barnes, president and CEO, and Janet Beard, vice president for community affairs, Fifth Third Bank Central Kentucky.

Philip R. McHugh, president & CEO, Fifth Third Bank Louisville and Mayor Bill Paxton, City of Paducah, Ky.

Like most Americans, I quickly tired of the drumbeat of crisis news coverage about everything from the abduction of children to celebrity breakdowns. Ultimately it has a numbing effect — we know too much and mental paralysis sets in. Many of us wind up doing what one CNN correspondent suggested: We go inside our houses at night, close the door and watch "reality" TV to escape the real reality.

Who knew the next step would be an around-the-clock source of information so vast that numbing doesn't begin to describe it? On the Internet we can get news updated every minute or so, read and analyze detailed government data online, download entire books and tap into encyclopedias and scholarly journals. Our virtual library seems to contain whatever we might need to make informed decisions about... well, about anything, including who we want to date, where we want to live, what kind of coffee-maker works best for the money (and where to buy it).

The online world has also allowed us to communicate instantly with each other without ever speaking a word (for that, we have our cell phones). And with these capabilities have come new opportunities for citizenship. We can "Google" the issues of the day, make campaign contributions online and sign letters of support or opposition that are written for us and will go directly to our elected representatives.

The down side is that all this technology gives us the false idea that we really know what's going on in the world — and that we're doing something about it. That's just not true.

Even in the Internet age, we're really no better informed about public life now than we were 20 years ago, according to a 2007 study by the Pew Research Center for People and the Press. This is the case even though our population has a much higher percentage of college graduates now — 27 percent compared to 17 percent in 1989.

Also, when we do use the Internet to learn more about public life, it's not guaranteed that we'll act on the information. Back in 2004, Democratic presidential candidate Howard Dean's campaign had great success stirring up online interest, but when it came time for the Democratic primaries, the interest didn't translate into votes. "In the end," said one Dean consultant, "a lot of the people who were brought into meet-ups and into virtual contact with one another turned out actually not to be particularly interested in electoral victory."

Connecting the dots, then, remains a challenge.

So many messages, so little time

Certainly having information at our fingertips is not a *bad* thing – not at all. The Pew research also found that the most informed of us are also more likely to vote and to believe that we have a personal stake in what goes on in public life. As city after city has learned the hard way, what we don't know about the way the world works today *will* hurt us.

But sitting at our computers, trolling for data, won't get the job done. The noted pollster Daniel Yankelovich has given a lot of thought to the way we make our minds up about, say, whom to vote for. He points out that in reality we just don't decide based on information alone.

First, he says, we "struggle hard" to align our opinions with our values. We also filter any information we receive through our personal "frames," or ways of perceiving the world. If forced to do so we then look at the trade-offs — if we do it my way, what will I, and we, have to give up?

Finally, he says, we must have time to work through our ideas, thoughts and emotions. This "working through" is "the very opposite of this notion of instant absorption," he says. He tells the story of the husband who comes home to two notes on the refrigerator from his wife. One says, "I'm leaving your dinner in the refrigerator." The other says, "I'm leaving you."

"The second note is shorter than the first, but it takes a lot more time to digest it," said Yankelovich.

Consider then that we are bombarded by an estimated 650 messages a day – through email, cell phones, the media. Not only could we never digest them all but they may distract us from the "working through" that's required if we're make decisions and act, whether about our personal lives or our communities.

Certainly there are still many times when that drumbeat of crisis coverage brings us together in a way nothing else can. During Hurricane Katrina we watched the utter breakdown of a city and its community, hour by hour. Because of what we learned in real time, many of us stepped forward to make a difference for New Orleans and southern Mississippi, knowing it could be our community the next time.

As always, it comes down to finding a balance — in this case between all the information we have available and our will and ability to act on it in the world, not just on the computer.

The loss of self

Probably the best-known work on community disconnection is *Bowling Alone* by Robert Putnam. He asserts that Americans have become increasingly isolated from each other and their communities since the advent of television, two-career families and the growth of suburbia. Putnam points to the decline in civic and social organizations and groups — the title refers to the fact that more people are bowling, but no longer in leagues.

Since *Bowling Alone* was published in 2000, some researchers have challenged Putnam's findings, pointing out that people are relating to each other in different ways — through email, for instance — definitions of civic participation may have changed in some ways for the better.

For instance, the civic pursuits of the 1950s and early 1960s weren't so much the result of "civic virtue deep in the soul" as a response to experience and opportunity in the wake of World War II, says Michael Schudson, a scholar of citizenship who is based at the University of California at San Diego. People who had pulled together for the war effort were again joining with one another, typically in homogenous groups that were segregated by gender and race.

This changed dramatically, of course, during the civil rights and women's rights movements of the 1960s. Among other things, citizens began to involve themselves in political decisions through protest activity.

And now, nearly 50 years later, civic involvement includes many more options than joining civic groups, voting or volunteering, Schudson says. Citizens may be gathering together for episodic events such as the million-mom and million-man marches and cultural events that help communities come to terms with an increasing Latino population. Such events have a longer-term impact on civic life than one might expect, he says.

What's more, many more of us are working for public or nonprofit human services organizations than were doing so 50 years ago; individuals and groups are more frequently pursuing social and environmental reforms through the courts; and in our homes and workplaces, there is more open and frank "everyday talk" about political and social issues.

Isolation and alienation

Yet there seems to be no question that in fundamental ways our social ties aren't as strong as they used to be, which will certainly affect the ways we relate to each other and work together.

"Instead of communities defined by close associations and deep commitments to family, friends and organizations, we seek places where we can make friends and acquaintances easily and live quasi-anonymous lives," Richard Florida writes. "The decline in the strength of our ties to people and institutions is a product of the increasing number of ties we have." And as with information overload, all those ties may overwhelm us without adding depth.

Indeed in 2004 Americans on average said they had only two confidants for important personal issues, compared to three in 1985. One-fourth of those surveyed said they had no one to talk to at all, according to the study from Duke University and University of Arizona sociologists.

Barry Wellman, a sociologist who studies networks and community and is based at the University of Toronto, says we are transitioning from traditional group life to "networked individualism." We are more independent and form relationships based on shared interests. Thus we affiliate based on our own choices rather than loyalty to a group, and our affiliations are easy to change.

A more disturbing finding comes from a follow-up study by Robert Putnam that suggests that diversity itself is causing people to withdraw from one another. The study found that the more diversity there is in a community, the less people vote, volunteer or participate in community projects. They also trust each other less regardless of whether they're the same ethnicity or not.

Putnam's study also found that those very cultural differences can be an advantage when it comes to problem solving. People looking at an issue from different perspectives may be more likely to come up with creative answers.

Still, the findings suggest that bringing citizens together around common concerns may be more complex than we realized.

And study after study reveals that we're becoming more alienated from politics as well. Perhaps we need no further statistical elaboration than the fact that the United States ranks close to the bottom among democracies in voter turnout. In focus groups we hear over and over: "My vote will make no difference" or "Those candidates won't help me" or "Why bother to go vote?"

And from the other side, many elected officials lament the fact that the only people who show up or speak out are those with extreme views on one side or another. Where, they ask, is the broad, silent middle?

Where is the hope?

As it turns out, the attack on the World Trade Center on Sept. 11, 2001, may have ultimately served to drive Americans further inside their tiny worlds.

This is in some ways a surprising result. As I recounted in *The Little Blue Book of Big Ideas*, one speaker observed that for an instant after 9/11, five things changed: little things mattered, little people mattered, authenticity mattered, people were saying hello in elevators and on the street and partisanship went out the window.

But most observers agree that we either did not take advantage of the opportunity to delve deeper into our connections as citizens or chose to ignore our communal needs and retreat once again into our living rooms.

Some point out that what we were left with after 9/11 was simply fear — and fear causes us to shut down, back away from each other and concentrate on our own survival.

But it's also true that engaging with each other, and with our communities, is the antidote to fear.

I like what Benjamin R. Barber of the Democracy Collaborative and University of Maryland said in a speech awhile back: "Fear, in fact, is engendered by spectatorship and passivity. That's a psychological reality. When you see an accident and you're standing on the sidewalk and simply stand and watch it — don't know about you, but with me, my heart's in my throat, my stomach's all upset, I'm fearful, I'm nervous, I'm anxious and the more I watch passively the more anxious I get.

"If you stop, jump up, help someone out of the car, give them mouth-to-mouth, try to get control of the traffic — the minute you get engaged, your fear is dispelled. Engagement and activity on the psychological level are the remedy to fear."

In fact we at the NewCities Institute are seeing that civic engagement at the community level, where citizens take action on behalf of a better quality of life, is becoming more attractive as world events move farther from our control.

This is quantifiable. One Harvard study of thousands of events in Chicago over the 30 years from 1970 to 2000 found that "civic engagement is durable overall," and that "blended social action" — meetings and other events combined with attempts to bring about change — was on the increase.

There are other encouraging signs. William Greider, national affairs correspondent for *The Nation,* asks in his essay "The Question of Power" whether Americans have it in them to reform some of the excesses of our capitalistic society.

"The broad public, I grant, doesn't look very promising, at least not the lumpy mass portrayed by the media," he writes.

"But people up close, like the folks I have encountered, represent the kind of purposeful minority that has always been the forerunner for deep change in our country — inventive and optimistic people, willing to commit to something larger than themselves and with a radical kind of patience."

In our view the key for communities will be building the connections to and among citizens that will encourage them to engage...and once engaged, to bring their skills, passions and love for the community to bear on its future. Hope alone is not enough, of course, but neither can we do without it. Wherever citizens engage with one another to build better communities, hope will flourish and thrive.

So what does the new citizenship — and citizen — look like? And how do we bring it about?

CHAPTER FIVE

CULTIVATING EVERYDAY HEROES AND A CITY'S COLLECTIVE WILL

Cities and citizens are interchangeable, as you can see — in today's world, you can't have one without another. A community survives and thrives based on the collective will of its people.

However, for too long our cities have played the "gotcha" game in which citizens blame leaders and leaders blame citizens.

Part of the reason is our expectations of each other. I like to say that instant coffee ruined the world; we tend to want immediate results with minimal effort. Citizens expect elected officials to act decisively to solve problems or seize opportunities. And elected officials expect citizens to educate themselves about local issues, attend public meetings and, for goodness sake, speak up!

Of course this isn't the way things work, and probably they never have, except perhaps in Frank Capra movies. Elected officials are justifiably nervous about making bold moves. The world is changing every day. What if that bold move takes our community off a cliff?

At the same time, citizens are understandably confused about what their role should be in public life. Sure we could attend public meetings. But when has that ever made a difference, really?

It's obvious to us at NewCities that neither elected officials nor citizens can make progress working alone. If we find ways to work together, we can hash out the advantages and trade-offs of those bold moves. And we're more likely to head off in the right direction if we have citizen input at the front end and support at the back end.

We've already talked about the importance of cities and communities focusing on the 12 Principles of Community Building, which we summarize as the Four P's: perspective, people, place and prosperity.

We've also looked at changes in community life and how they affect the civic engagement: we can live and work wherever we want, we are on the whole more isolated and independent, and we are likely to be overwhelmed — and turned off — by the barrage of news and information that's available around the clock.

So how do we make all this come together for community building? At the NewCities Institute we've settled on three important steps for communities, their leaders and citizens:

- Becoming informed...in order to see the possible
- Being inclusive...because leadership springs from everywhere

- Exerting leadership...because it's required in big and small ways

Being informed...in order to see the possible

I've already discussed the down side of information overload. So why am I emphasizing now that we must be informed?

In the context of community building being informed means understanding your community's strengths and weaknesses, its challenges and opportunities, locally and on a global scale. The 12 Principles of Community Building provide a framework for this understanding.

However a bigger question is how to share that information — from elected leaders to citizens and vice versa — so everyone knows what he or she needs to know.

Heretofore, there's been a tacit agreement in public life that sharing some information with citizens can be counterproductive. This has often been the case in economic development when industries considering a particular location want everything kept quiet.

But today's technology means there are no secrets, even when companies are considering relocating — and especially when communities are considering their options for developing an economic strategy. Data galore are on the web. Gossip can be transmitted instantly and in Technicolor. Recently I noticed a sign at Gold's Gym, where I go to exercise, forbidding the use of cell phones. Some of the members were taking surreptitious photos from their camera phones and transmitting them to friends. All I can think is how desperate those "friends" must be!

For the very most part, however, sharing information about the options and trade-offs involved in local government decisions is the most effective way to ensure that we can "see the possible" and make solid decisions about what alternatives to pursue. The issues are complex and, if citizens are to be engaged, they need to understand them.

I remember reading about the approach of Menlo Park, Calif., when citizens came to a meeting upset about the city's plan to cut services. City officials handed out budget sheets to the citizens. Once they could look at the numbers, line by line, the conversation became more reasonable.

Two-way communication

The other side of the coin is that communicating this information goes both ways. Citizens must be willing to share their own knowledge, values and beliefs — *and* be willing to compromise. Local government and civic leaders must likewise be willing to consider what they've heard.

Again, cities and communities have shied away from this approach many times because it just seems that asking citizens for input results in a venting session with lots of uninformed opinion. Who needs that?

However we're talking about a different kind of dialogue: a structured, ongoing conversation that will lead to productive results about what a community values and how it will make decisions about its future.

The thing is, once a community has mastered this process, it can use the process again and again for many purposes. If one "bold move" doesn't work out, the community already knows how to map out another one.

This may sound like the obvious thing to do. It's not. That's because of another perceived drawback: the time it takes for a thoughtful community conversation. Often we believe that we need to act right away before too much opposition develops or before opportunity passes us by. Talk about our instant coffee mentality!

But real, lasting change often is a back-and-forth, time-consuming process, even in today's world. Daniel Kemmis, the Missoula mayor, said that in his experience, political change is not linear but dialectical.

"There may be times when we sail with the wind of history full astern; but the more common, the more challenging and, frankly, the more interesting experience is more akin to tacking, moving forward by bringing the wind now on the port, now on the starboard bow."

Talking about more than the facts

One last point about being informed is that we do not learn and act based on facts alone. Facts certainly help, but sharing stories from personal experience are just as critical. True stories breathe life into issues that otherwise might seem too remote to urgently solve. They help us understand where another person is coming from and how we might find common ground. A story makes our concerns more vivid and inspires us to work together. It cues the emotional responses that are the primary motivator of individual and organizational change.

This doesn't mean that stories are simply the "spoonful of sugar that makes the medicine go down." They're part of the larger truth that we as citizens and civic leaders must understand as we contemplate our community's future.

The importance of sharing stories has been affirmed in recent years by authors and thinkers such as Daniel Pink in *A Whole New Mind*, which explores the importance of using both left-brain and right-brain intelligence to compete in today's world; Lori Silverman in *Wake Me When the Data is Over* that showcases more than 70 organizations which are achieving tangible, bottom-line results through the use of story in myriad business applications; and a new magazine, *Digital Communities,* which is advancing the notion that technological developments alone are empty without the idea of community and applications to improve the quality of life.

But I first heard about the importance of using stories a dozen years ago in a discussion with the mayor of Burkesville, Ky. A former army general, the mayor listened as I marveled about the many colorful, interesting and gifted people who held elective office that I met through the Kentucky League of Cities. I had a sense that the stories they told about choosing a life of pubic service could do far more than help the public understand government and government leaders. Such stories could build trust and a genuine connection and tolerance for opposing views that is necessary for democracy to flourish. But intrigued as I was, I had no time to reflect on the stories, much less write about them. The mayor offered a simple suggestion.

"You might be busy, but take the time to carry index cards and write down the vignettes of those you come into contact with," he said. "You'll return to those cards someday, and they will be more valuable than you realize."

Keeping those words in mind, I was amazed at how my ears became more attuned to stories that had been right under my nose. I have gone so far as to incorporate the use of story in Kentucky League of Cities and NewCities Institute policy by assigning a database for their collection and disseminating them throughout our work. Thus when we at NewCities learn of everyday people doing extraordinary things to make their communities better, we are able to share their stories to inspire others.

Whether it's organizational work or community building, stories connect us in profound ways that go beyond mere intellect and get to the deeper currents that move us to reflection and action. Hearing that our community must do more to meet the needs of immigrants is one thing, but consider the difference when it is the story of a specific immigrant family, their challenges and contributions.

Being inclusive...because leadership can spring from anywhere

Often in citizen engagement efforts, elected leaders tap the "usual suspects" — people who already have made a contribution to the community, or who have a position that identifies them as stakeholders (chamber of commerce president, etc.).

What we've learned at NewCities, though, is how important it is to widen the net to pull in people who may have different perspectives to offer: young people, people of different ethnicities, retirees, singles, everybody.

This isn't just because people need to feel included. It's because community building requires all forms of citizen participation. Citizen A might invest in the local economy by starting a small business while Citizen B might join a local government committee to map out a strategic plan. Other forms of participation include one-time acts of courage, such as speaking out when no one else dares, and long-term commitments, such as running for local office.

Being inclusive is also important because community building must be done by the people who are going to live with the consequences.

We know based on assorted analyses that America's population is getting older, yet Generation Y — born between 1977 to 1995 — is by some accounts larger than the baby boomer generation, which is starting to retire.

Because of immigration, an increasing number of citizens may also speak a different language or come from a different culture than the norm in our community.

And because of our changing society, he or she may be a traditional civic leader or activist. Or he or she may go about things independently, eschewing the usual committee memberships or volunteer work.

As I said in the introduction, the citizens who become everyday heroes do not just engage in good works. They are true "citizens" who defy labels such as conservative and liberal, choosing instead to roll up their sleeves and make the world a better place one community at a time. Among other things, they have a deep sense of caring for others and doing the right thing, which may put them at odds with their fellows and friends; a desire to encourage others and seek others' ideas; a certain conflict about decisions that are difficult but must be made; and a passion for results and for making a measurable difference.

Consider these citizens who have made a difference in their own unique ways:

- Gary Dunham, a retired Republican businessman, saw Democrat Al Gore's documentary *An Inconvenient Truth* on a trip to Washington with his wife, according to *Time* magazine. Gripped by its call to action to protect our environment, Dunham started telling everyone he knew about the documentary, and he was the first of more than 1,200 people to be trained to show it to others in their communities.

- Lynette Bybee of Flagstaff, Ariz., the young woman who wanted help talking to her mayor, is today offering temporary shelter to hundreds of homeless people at a hotel that accepts vouchers from local charitable organizations. Her private sector, for-profit approach has raised legitimate questions from public officials and nonprofit providers. But it has also spotlighted the needs of the homeless and advanced local partnerships about how to meet them.

- A group of twenty-something kayakers in Missoula, Mont., spent years going through the bureaucratic process in order to create a river feature known as "Brennan's Wave" in honor of a friend who died. Their efforts were a potential boost for the local tourism industry. What's more, the young boating enthusiasts developed "civic virtues like patience and perseverance, teamwork, a capacity for give-and-take, the ability to stay in relationships with people whose seeming wrong-headedness and narrow-mindedness they could barely endure," according to former Mayor Daniel Kemmis.

Other times citizens who "engage" don't start out with any big plan, just an idea that they want to make things better. In 2006 businesswoman Carol Cespedes, who lives outside Austin, Tx., invited her neighbors over to talk about the kind of public controversy that tends to bring folks together: a road-building project that would affect their neighborhood of a hundred homes called South Windmill Run.

Once they started working together around the road project, though, the neighbors got interested in addressing everything from car burglaries to cleanup and restoration of the local park. They formed a neighborhood association that is still active. "We still have our share of political issues," Cespedes wrote in a recent newsletter, "but we have the means for expressing the will of the neighborhood. Better still, we have a neighborhood with a will to be expressed!"

Young people

Perhaps the biggest challenge — and opportunity — in civic engagement is involving young people who perceive their roles and responsibilities in their communities differently than local leaders may be used to.

There are encouraging signs that our younger citizens are ready to participate:

- They turned out to vote in historically high numbers in the 2004 presidential election, according to the Center for Information and Research on Civic Learning and Engagement at the University of Maryland.
- Seventy-seven percent of college students voted, and college students "were more likely to participate than many other groups in American society," the center reported.
- According to another study, voting by young minorities also increased, including an 11 percent jump among African-Americans age 18 to 24.

CULTIVATING EVERYDAY HEROES AND A CITY'S COLLECTIVE WILL

These young people are part of Generation Y, whose members have been the subject of many studies and profiles because of their impact on the workforce.

Generation Y was described recently in *Fortune* magazine as ambitious, demanding and questioning of everything, "so if there isn't a good reason for that long commute or late night, don't expect them to do it. When it comes to loyalty, the companies they work for are last on their list — behind their families, their friends, their communities, their co-workers, and, of course, themselves."

Some suggest this translates into "the end of authority" in the American workplace. Yet traditional expectations about roles and responsibilities are deeply ingrained, particularly in older generations. I remember my first job out of law school. I was working in Florida and left the office at 3 p.m. one day to give my parents a tour of my new hometown. My dad, a veteran of factory work, was surprised to see me that early in the day, wondering whether my boss had actually let me leave work before the usual time.

That was still the era, even in the 1960s and 1970s, when authority mattered. Some people think of them as the good old days when people knew who was the boss and did as they were told. People like my World War II-era father just didn't question those who were in charge.

Yet those kinds of questions are a central part of community building, even as it's also important to defer at times to the people who have been elected to make the final decisions. This will be the challenge for Generation Y.

Certainly the young will find their own way. They're more likely to connect through social networking sites such as MySpace and FaceBook, which allow daily collaboration. And hundreds of thousands of them from around the world have visited TakingITGlobal.org, an online community that helps young people connect with each other to find inspiration. They are getting involved and taking action in their local and global communities.

Others are combining old and new ways of approaching civic life, as they are in the tiny community of Inez, Ky. This is the town where, in 1963, President Lyndon Johnson declared the war on poverty in a famous front-porch appearance with an Appalachian family.

Forty years later, the statistics are discouraging: Inez has fewer than 500 people, and about one-third of them live in poverty. The town center is run down. Inez is losing its young people and drugs are a scourge there as they are in small towns throughout America. Jobs are scarce, with the only hopeful sign being an up-tick in coal mining.

What gives me hope, however, is that Generations X and Y are assuming leadership roles there. On a recent visit I became acquainted with the mayor, in his mid-thirties, who had run for office to turn things around; a councilman who kept me from my lunch to drill me with questions about revitalizing downtown, growing the city and stopping the drugs; and the woman who runs the Roy F. Collier Community Center. The center is an amazing place with fitness facilities, an award-winning day care center and first-run movie theater all under one roof.

Of course there's no way to know if this generation's answers will take hold.

On the other hand, it's also possible they'll take hold more effectively than previous generations' answers did.

Exerting leadership...because it's required in big and small ways

On one day my mother would say, "The early bird gets the worm!" and the next day, "Measure twice, cut once!" I remember wondering which was more important, jumping at an opportunity or wading in with utmost caution. It seems the advice you get, even from your mother, can leave you pretty conflicted.

And so it is with community building. Sometimes the key seems to be the steady work of stalwart citizens on the local councils and chambers of commerce and Rotary clubs. These true everyday heroes give countless hours to community projects that may take years to complete.

Yet it also seems essential to take bold action, and that requires visionary leaders who challenge others to see the possible.

The proposed Museum Plaza in Louisville, Ky., for instance, is a great project in and of itself, but more so because it fits into Mayor Jerry Abramson's vision for how Louisville Metro can become a competitive, top-tier American city. The architecturally unique skyscraper development will tie together downtown museums and feature condominiums, restaurants and even the University of Louisville's master of fine arts program. There's no question that a visionary approach to community building can make a tremendous difference.

Still, the most successful elected officials remember that it will take many small steps and unsung heroes to make the project a reality – and almost anything worthwhile will take some time.

For instance, Richmond, Ky., is fast becoming an international city because of the vision of Mayor Connie Lawson. She says that Richmond's international focus is only fitting: the city is the home of a major regional university, Eastern Kentucky University (EKU), which attracts international students.

But Mayor Lawson has also kept an eye on the little things that might get in the way of her vision. Finding that a disproportionate share of international students were having confrontations with law enforcement officers, for instance, she looked at the reasons why. A big reason was poor communication, which did not surprise her. "Wouldn't we Kentuckians have the same problem if plucked down in the middle of a foreign country," she asked?

As part of her proposed solution, Mayor Lawson took a key small step. In partnership with EKU the city created laminated identification cards for international students that include, among other things, the mayor's name and cell phone number to call in an emergency.

This was not only a "little thing" to advance Mayor Lawson's vision of an international city but the kind of thing a community patriot does: being willing to work one-on-one, day-to-day to make longer term changes.

Of course integrating a community's vision with the "little things" is more art than science. That's the challenge for leaders who take on both. It's not uncommon for busy public servants to lose sight of the big picture or see a project fail because of lack of attention to detail.

But those kinds of mistakes also teach local leaders to appreciate the importance of both. In fact, it's sometimes hard to know which will make the most difference at the end of the day. Often we think it's "the vision thing," but that's not always true.

I often tell the story of my mother's final days when a Hospice doctor said to her, "You need to tell me what you like to do so I can adjust your medication and allow you to do it better."

She replied in a soft but resolute voice, "I like to do little things."

Adding it all up to the "intentional city"

In our view, at the NewCities Institute, being informed, being inclusive and exerting leadership are the essential elements of what we call an "intentional city." Hope alone won't suffice.

With an engaged citizenry, a more holistic view of the city's problems and needs is possible. In an intentional city citizens are far more active in shaping their city's personality and planning its future.

People have more reason to come together in city life more purposefully now because many of them have the ability to live and work anywhere they wish. Quality of life becomes important. At the same time, they have enormous power to define the city and attend to the hardware that helps ensure economic and social security.

Intent and involvement are everything. Once in place, a true New City can emerge.

CHAPTER SIX

AMERICA'S FIRST NEWCITY: MOSCOW, IDAHO

The early history of Moscow, Idaho, suggests a certain lightheartedness among the settlers. Perhaps they were just giddy at their good fortune: they'd found gently rolling hills of fertile soil that proved ideal for growing wheat, and soon the railroads came along to connect their part of the world with everyplace else. Some of those original citizens wanted to name their little city Hog Heaven because pigs liked to feast on its wild camas bulbs (long a staple of Native Americans who traversed the area). Later, Fourth of July celebrations included a race to see who was the town's fastest fat man.

A hundred years later Moscow citizens still enjoy a variety of community celebrations, but growth and competing interests have caused them to take things more seriously, at least when it comes to their city's future. The community is almost evenly divided between the political right and left. This was evident in the results of the 2004 presidential race when Democrat John Kerry defeated Republican President George Bush in the City of Moscow while the county as a whole went for Bush.

Political division has long manifested itself in local discussions about growth and development. "Some Moscow citizens believe the town is perfect just as it is, said Mayor Nancy Chaney, while others say it must build and grow or die. "I think reality is somewhere between," she said.

A special place

Regardless of their political persuasions Moscow citizens agree on one thing: They live in a special place — the breathtaking Palouse region of northern Idaho and eastern Washington. The Palouse is dryland farm country with rich loess soil, hypnotic and beautiful above the Snake River plain.

Moscow itself, a town of about 22,000 people, is home to the University of Idaho, the state's major research institution with an enrollment of approximately 12,000 students. It is just eight miles east of Washington State University in Pullman, Wash. Moscow's tree-lined downtown historic district is quaint and inviting, and the community boasts 17 neighborhood parks. Residents and visitors enjoy Moscow's vibrant arts community and outdoor recreation opportunities.

Like so many small towns in the West, Moscow is relatively isolated. The nearest big city, Spokane, Wash., is more than an hour away. Growth in the Palouse region has been slow and steady, but as farmland turns to development, concerns have arisen about sprawl and traffic. Debates related to growth and development are often energetic and sometimes divisive. When the city council considered an ordinance to regulate "big-box" stores, for instance, one group of citizens rallied to support it while another opposed it.

Idaho is generally a conservative state, but Moscow has a comparatively more liberal-minded population of citizens connected to the university. Two citizen action groups have come to the fore, the Moscow Civic Association (MCA) and the Greater Moscow Alliance (GMA), representing decidedly different perspectives, particularly regarding growth and development.

"Like many towns, Moscow residents fall into a lot of different categories," Council President Linda Pall said. "Some are quite conservative and see themselves as the reddest of the red. Others see themselves as progressives or liberals on town issues as well as their personal lives. Of course we have some thoroughly libertarian folks who would limit city government to city utilities, police and fire, period."

Planning for change

By 2004 Moscow's elected leaders decided that it was time to revise the city's comprehensive plan to update the collective vision of the community and provide long range planning for growth and development.

Citizen surveys indicated that the lack of good paying jobs was a major concern. The challenge was how to best encourage employers to locate or expand businesses in Moscow while protecting the quality of life that residents were passionate about.

At a city council retreat members agreed that they needed to find a way to encourage broader citizen participation in general and to provide for more productive community discussion regarding public issues such as the comprehensive plan.

About that time Pall attended a National League of Cities conference where she learned about the NewCities approach to citizen engagement. NewCities was looking for a place to pilot its 12 Principles of Community Building, and Moscow's participation would bring it positive publicity. Perhaps this would be the way to foster more citizen participation, Pall said.

"We continued to be interested in economic development, but we continued to have voices in the community who wanted to go in all different directions," Pall said.

"It's a real challenge for city leadership to bring everyone together and get everyone to talk about their desires and wants and needs and try to create a whole that makes some sense."

People

The NewCities team began its work in Moscow by meeting with many local groups to foster a sense of inclusiveness. There was a kick-off event in the town square that brought out 500 people. "Early on I think the NewCities folks were all hoping that this was just going to be a seamless, smooth ride," Chaney said.

But it would not be so easy.

Citizens were invited to participate in a *charrette*, or a process for exploring land-use planning issues. At a *charrette* citizens are effectively put in the driver's seat and challenged to devise visions for enhancing and protecting the community's economic, environmental and social well-being.

The *charrette* only attracted 50 or 60 people, and most of those came from what they would probably describe as a "progressive liberal" point of view, Pall said. The group was not monolithic — it ran the gamut from people who wanted no growth to people who just wanted sensible limits on sprawl. But "the pro-growth people stayed away," Pall said. "So the results of that meeting were not entirely reflective of the community as a whole."

The local newspaper reported the disappointing turnout. NewCities and Moscow leaders reached out to the Greater Moscow Alliance and other pro-growth advocates who were not convinced that their perspective would genuinely be considered and incorporated in the NewCities work.

They attended a follow-up meeting to discuss the themes that emerged in the *charrette* and a community-wide "listening session," and they did not like what had been done so far.

"It was like divorce court where the wife's advocates were on one side of the courtroom, the husband's on the other, and people who had not taken sides not knowing where to sit!" Pall said.

Finding common ground

The benefit, however, was that the follow-up conversation had everyone's attention, Pall said. About 200 people attended. "Some people would say it was terrible. But it was very good that we had the conflict. We met the 'elephant in the room' that no one really wanted to acknowledge."

When everyone started talking it became clear that sides were not as divided as they may have appeared. "The groups overlapped a fair amount in the middle, but the extremes in both groups got the headlines."

Ultimately NewCities suggested that, to preserve Moscow's advantages while also encouraging local development, the city should grow "in" and not "out" by reclaiming abandoned lots and adding housing — even highrises — that would be within walking distance of downtown and the university.

Not everybody liked all of the suggestions — especially the high-rise idea — but that wasn't the point. Moscow citizens were beginning to see that there were many possibilities to choose from and that they might be able to agree on a few and make some progress.

They were also motivated because of the "underlying optimism and 'can do' attitude" that is behind the NewCities philosophy of community building, Chaney said. Moscow's struggles had left its citizens uncertain at times about its prospects. "Community building is not just about infrastructure. It's a very emotional subject," Chaney said. "We care so much about this place."

Perspective and prosperity

That optimism extended to discussions about the Palouse Knowledge Corridor, which came about after Moscow stepped back to gain some perspective on its position in the region.

The thing is, Moscow really isn't as isolated as it first would seem. When citizens talked about what they valued about the community they often singled out the University of Idaho, its research and technological capabilities and worldwide connectedness in today's virtual environment.

Washington State University, in Pullman, Wash., is only eight miles away. And with the exception of the Research Triangle Park in North Carolina, there probably is not another place in rural America where research capacity, brain power and quality of life are as concentrated, NewCities observed.

However, the University of Idaho has often looked south toward the state capital and the rest of the state for opportunities to collaborate while Washington State University looked west to Olympia and the population centers in western Washington. What if they began focusing more attention on each other with the idea of developing a "Knowledge Corridor" in the emerging economic super region of the Pacific Northwest?

The idea wasn't exactly new, but it had been "waxing and waning in a loose-knit fashion for years," Chaney said. When NewCities included it among the options for the community to consider, it gained traction largely because of the context. Citizens were saying that they didn't want smokestacks or sprawl, but they did want better jobs and general economic prosperity. A knowledge corridor seemed like an obvious and promising next step.

Expanding the possibilities

Chaney and the NewCities team approached the two university presidents who agreed to collaborate on a commission to develop plans for the corridor. The idea would be to connect the universities, in Moscow and Pullman, in ways that could benefit start-up businesses and technology companies.

Synergy was created quickly, Chaney said, because both universities were expanding their work in the area of the sustainability. Among other things that meant constructing buildings that were energy efficient and water conserving, thus saving on heating, cooling and water costs. High-profile developers in other parts of Idaho are now constructing such buildings, and local developers have become interested as well. The City of Moscow is now collaborating with the University of Idaho on a project aimed at building sustainable communities; it even has a sustainability intern and a sustainability line item in its budget.

This might be one of those issues that divided the citizens who differ on growth and development issues. The question of protecting the environment versus promoting growth has been so sensitive in the past that when the idea of a "ring road" and bypass came up some in the community favored a parkway with paths to form a sort of greenbelt around the city instead.

But the very public discussions about the knowledge corridor and city and university sustainability initiatives have helped convince the community that "economic well being and environmental responsibility are not mutually exclusive," Chaney said.

In the meantime, the county's economic development council has hired a marketing firm to help "brand" the knowledge corridor with a logo and slogan and the local schools have already agreed to include it on their stationery.

Place

When citizens came together to discuss what they valued about Moscow as the place they choose to live and its quality of life several themes emerged. Among other things, they wanted to keep the small town atmosphere, bridge the town-gown divide, grow without sprawl and tame the car.

Moscow was already making headway in some of these areas and the idea was to build momentum. Thus a town that was already considered pedestrian-friendly was encouraged to develop even more paths and sidewalks for bicyclists and pedestrians. The "strip" could be beautified with more green space. More affordable housing could be provided downtown where residents could get around without driving and adding to the traffic problems.

The high-rise idea from NewCities went over like a lead balloon. But soon, an urban renewal effort began in the deteriorating railroad industrial area at the edge of downtown. Next, two local architects and educators acquired a complex of seven agricultural buildings on a prominent corner between the campus and downtown adjacent to a popular produce shop. Their early vision was to work with the exteriors to create a quirky, artsy set of mixed-use buildings that would provide retail and office space, housing, a climbing wall and potentially a unique space for research in the round inside an old grain elevator.

"One of the things that we're doing there is getting people involved at a grassroots level," Pall said. "Property owners are involved in a meaningful way in getting urban planning going."

Back to the comprehensive plan

At the same time the city began work on its comprehensive plan, developing an extensive public input process that included dozens of neighborhood discussions as well as community-wide meetings and household surveys.

"We've gradually been honing our abilities to do a good job at these meetings," Chaney said. That means becoming more effective at soliciting citizen input and also at analyzing that input so it can be useful.

Elected officials also made communications a priority among the city, county and community agencies so they can learn from and build on each other's ideas and projects. "We're not making as many compartmentalized decisions," Chaney said. "If there are ways of benefiting the broader community by piggy-backing projects and leveraging resources, the city wants to make sure that happens." That was a key part of the NewCities message, she said: "It's all connected."

And yet the increased efforts to communicate with citizens about government plans and decisions also had unexpected benefits. In May 2007 the city experienced a tragedy when a county resident went on a shooting spree downtown, killing three people and wounding others before shooting himself. In the midst of the crisis the city and county made it a priority to communicate with citizens as quickly as possible about what had happened and what was being done about it.

"The idea was to remind the community that this event was uncommon, that we are here to help each other to build a safe, caring place, but we're not immune to the violence around the world," Chaney said.

Several citizens told her they felt reassured, she said. "They were proud of our community, that we were focusing on the positive and trying to address the problem in a coordinated way.

"We are a community, first and foremost. When it comes down to helping each other, we are there," Chaney said.

Pall put it this way: "The problems the city has had before are still there. However, we have real tools that we are using to meet those challenges and a new sense of purpose. That intense year of working through this...the reality of it was that we got to look seriously at our future and look at the ways in which we wanted to act and the way we wanted to shape that future and not just be acted upon."

"It was all about a street project."
Council President Linda Pall

Linda Pall says she is hardwired for civic involvement.

"It goes back to beating up a kid on a playground when I was 6-years-old for dissing Adlai Stevenson," she said with a laugh.

"I come from a family that is very, very committed to public service. The idea that you give back to the community is just the way it is. My heroine, when I grew up, was Eleanor Roosevelt."

Pall wasn't too far past her playground days when she started getting involved in more formal ways. As a teenager she worked on the 1960 Kennedy presidential campaign. She was in her early twenties and teaching at Portland State University in 1970 when she was appointed to Oregon's first Women's Commission.

She also got married that year, and in 1972 moved to Moscow, Idaho, because her husband had accepted a teaching job just across the state line in Pullman, Wash. As was her nature, Pall was involved in Moscow's downtown planning issues before some of us would have unpacked our boxes.

"I immediately thought, 'Wow, we have lots to do here. Moscow is just the perfect place to do it,'" she said. "I could be put down any place and in two days I'd have something organized."

In this case, she said, "It was all about a street project."

There was a proposal for a one-way couplet downtown, meaning two streets would each become one way in opposite directions. That was all fine, except the traffic had to rejoin on both ends. That would involve tearing down housing and, in Pall's mind, causing other problems. She thought an exterior bypass was really what the town needed, and as a new resident she didn't hesitate to say so.

She didn't win. The couplet was built, but she and others like her did succeed in getting the ends redesigned in a way that would have less negative impact. The experience also launched her into the heart of downtown revitalization issues.

Pall had a son, Zach, in 1974, and during the rest of that decade she balanced multiple roles. She was home with Zach during his preschool years and helped found a preschool and kindergarten called the Moscow Day School.

She finished her master's degree in political science and later earned her Ph.D. And she was elected to the city council in 1977, just five years after moving to town.

Pall served on the council until 1983 when she stepped down because of personal and professional demands.

A divorce, a career change (she went to law school, got a degree and built a law practice) and the continued demands of parenting took most of her attention for awhile. "My son was my number one priority," she said.

But Zach graduated from high school in June 1993 and by that fall, she was again running for city council. She was re-elected and has served ever since — except for two years that she jokingly refers to as a "brief electoral hiatus."

In her role on the council, Pall has been no stranger to conflict. The NewCities process itself generated "a lot of letters to the editor." But conflict is necessary if you're truly going to bring everyone to the table, she said.

"I believe that a direct approach is generally the best," she said. "I say, 'Marshal your best argument, get your evidentiary ducks in a row, count your direct supporters, assess your indirect supporters, be realistic about your opponents and try to resolve the matter.' The worst-case scenarios come when there are pressures to avoid, postpone, divert, etc."

"When the conflict is personal, my preference is to ignore it if at all possible," she added. It's important, she said, to get past opinions "to what the real issue is. Perhaps that person doesn't understand your position or doesn't have all the information." Or it may be that there's a personality conflict. There are times, she said, when "your only alternative is to pull the Miss America smile out of your backpack, paste it on and move ahead hopefully."

~~~

Linda is tireless in her efforts to understand all sides of an issue and *still* find a way to move forward – bringing other people with her. She may be strong-minded, but she's also incredibly tolerant of other views, an essential element of citizenship – and leadership – in the 21st century.

"In a small town like this, things don't happen unless you make them happen."

Judy Brown

Judy Brown was 22 with a new degree in chemistry when she joined the Peace Corps and traveled to Kenya to teach math and science for two years.

"It was a really a wonderful experience," she said. She brought home with her a new perspective on what it means to live in a place you're not from. "I didn't want to be an expatriate in a place where I didn't really belong," she said. "I wanted to put down some roots."

That desire was tested when she moved to Moscow, Idaho, in 1987. It was the smallest town she had ever lived in.

She was, in the jargon of the relocation industry, a "trailing spouse" to her husband, who was joining the faculty at the University of Idaho. In those early years in Moscow she was trying to finish a dissertation on the changing roles of county extension agents while raising young children. She quickly got involved in their schools, but it took her a while to make true friends.

"One of the first things I noticed when I got here," she said, "was that everybody knew everybody, but their relationships often were not particularly deep."

That was, she believed, precisely because everybody knew everybody. People were more careful about what they revealed about themselves when they knew that what one person knew, everyone might soon know.

Gradually, of course, she did find friends. And one of those, the director of the local library, asked Brown for help with an effort to revive a long-dormant Friends of the Library group.

Soon, she was also involved in a local environmental institute and the League of Women Voters.

"I started realizing that in a small town like this, things don't happen unless you make them happen," she said.

The community involvement has been rewarding for Brown in many ways. Not only has it strengthened her ties with Moscow and given her that sense of belonging she vowed to have, it also helped her to re-enter the full-time workforce when her children were older. The League of Women Voters led to her involvement in a study of welfare reform. That enabled her to eventually find a job working with a nonprofit based in Boise called United Vision for Idaho.

But perhaps her most successful citizen effort came when she agreed to serve on the city-sponsored Paradise Path Task Force, which created a series of walking paths through Moscow.

Her involvement came about simply. City Council member Linda Pall asked her to do it. She had no particular expertise other than her ability to help with grant applications and publicity. "I do walk," she said. "And it's my main form of exercise, so I am passionate about it in that way."

But mostly, "I just thought the idea was really neat."

Essentially, Brown and others have had to retrofit a system of paths into a city that was already established, and that took time.

But 14 years later, Moscow has approximately five miles of pathways connecting the city and its parks, including a sensory garden with paths that are handicapped-accessible.

Some of the pathways link up with routes that go out of the city — to Pullman, Wash., and to Troy, Idaho. Some follow a creek and also involve converted rail rights-of-way. And some are nothing more than sections of paved road in quiet neighborhoods that have been identified as a safe place to walk.

As the task force moves forward with its work, it is doing so with increasing input from Moscow residents about what they need and want from their neighborhoods – including input they received from the NewCities process.

Brown has gotten a lot out of becoming an active member of Moscow, but ultimately her reasons for doing so are simply because it's right.

"I just feel like a citizen has a responsibility to give back to the community," she said.

I've met many everyday heroes like Judy. They may think they possess no singular talent, yet they step forward to participate, learn the ropes and persist until they are leading the way. Their dependability and determination inspire others, who ultimately stick it out with them!

CHAPTER SEVEN

KENTUCKY'S FIRST NEWCITY: MOREHEAD, KENTUCKY

Like a fairy tale sleeping giant, Morehead, Ky., has for decades been tucked into the foothills of the Daniel Boone National Forest, relaxed and comfortable as the small town home of a state university with many advantages:

- it is located on an interstate, making it more attractive to industrial prospects than many similar-sized towns in Eastern Kentucky;
- Cave Run Lake and the national forest provide abundant tourism opportunities; and
- the community has a downtown conference center, regional hospital and a strong public school system.

But until 2006 Morehead had not roused itself to build on those advantages, though it had at times addressed specific disadvantages.

In the 1990s, for instance, many small cities in Kentucky began focusing on their downtowns that were declining partly because of competition from big-box stores on the city outskirts. In 1998 civic leaders created an organization — Morehead Tomorrow — to take the lead on downtown revitalization. Results included the conference center, and residents were delighted.

At the same time, Mayor Brad Collins said, it was just "a one-phase project for downtown with little or no citizen input."

A new direction

As the "information age" emerged after the turn of the 21st century, community leaders became concerned about sustaining the local economy in a time of globalization. Should Morehead branch out in new directions or build on existing efforts? What would the trade-offs be?

Local government officials revised Morehead's comprehensive plan, but, in order to make any major changes, they realized they would need to have more citizen participation.

However, local government had always operated on the assumption that "elected officials do what is best for the citizens," Collins said. "We had never had any long-range citizen involvement." Whenever there was a need for short-term involvement, he said, "we would always choose who we wanted to be involved."

So how were they going to change that mindset? Collins knew about the NewCities Institute because he was active in the Kentucky League of Cities, which started the institute. And NewCities was eager to begin a pilot project in civic engagement with a willing community in its home state of Kentucky.

But Collins wasn't sure at first how willing he was for NewCities to get involved. For one thing, what would Morehead citizens say if the city spent good money on consultants just to get them talking? And once they started talking, would he and other elected officials have to listen endlessly to all they'd done wrong?

"They had to drag me into this. I was really worried about it," Collins said. "We had never listened for a long time to what the citizens wanted. It scared me a little bit."

Collins began to gain confidence when the county, the medical center and university all agreed to help the city fund the NewCities project. It turned out that the idea of collaborating with citizens and each other on the community's future was appealing to everyone.

"That was a miracle to get everyone to put in the money," Collins said.

"But the bigger miracle was the level and quality of citizen involvement. I never dreamed of having this much," he said.

Listening to the community

At the first "community building session" on a Thursday evening organizers set up 400 chairs thinking that was optimistic. More than 500 people showed up, and it was standing room only. Collins saw the turnout as a "direct reaction to people feeling like they would be heard."

"We want to listen to you," was the message to the citizens, Collins said. "And they made it clear up front that if they were going to tell community leaders what to focus on, they expected those leaders to respond."

At the same time the barrage of criticism that Collins had feared did not come about, though there were times when he and other elected officials "had to bite our tongues a bit."

For the next two months hundreds of citizens and civic leaders gathered at a total of six forums throughout Rowan County and Morehead to discuss what they valued about the community and what they wanted and needed from their leaders.

Usually, said Dudley Herron, a retired Morehead State University (MSU) professor who served on the NewCities project committee, the same people tended to show up at community meetings — people like him. Because of its medical center and university, Morehead has a lot of well-educated, outspoken professionals who, Herron said, value "progress, whatever progress is."

But there is another group of longer-term residents who know and value the region's history and find growth somewhat frightening, Herron said. They are the turkey hunters, the bluegrass musicians, the storytellers. That group often stays quiet because they don't expect anyone to listen.

"We were concerned," he remembered. "How do you get input from that segment of the community?"

One strategy was to hold the forums at volunteer fire stations, which have tremendous support from a broad spectrum of people, and often host community events and fundraisers like fish fries, Herron said.

"There's a sense of community surrounding many of those places," he said. People who aren't used to participating in more formal types of civic engagement *are* accustomed to participating in events at the fire stations.

The community also held a meeting on the Morehead State campus. "We didn't get as many students as we would have liked," Herron said, "but we did get input from that segment of the community that we would not have gotten if we had not gone there."

At each of the sessions people's comments were written down and recorded so that everyone attending would know their views were being accurately conveyed. Then, NewCities would look for the common themes and report back to the community.

More agreement than disagreement

The idea of the listening sessions was to gather perspectives from a variety of Morehead residents; but as it turned out, residents agreed more than they disagreed.

They wanted more and better jobs, and yet they also wanted to preserve Morehead's small town atmosphere and Appalachian heritage. "We take care of each other," they said, as well as, "We take what we have for granted."

Residents also wanted to revitalize downtown, enhance the local environment, increase tourism and improve government efficiency.

"It was enlightening and surprising to see that the views and ideas from all areas were the same," said Rodney Hitch, executive director of the Morehead-Rowan County Economic Development Council.

By the end of it all the community had not only assessed its priorities but had started talking about how to move forward on them. Here's how its work broke down in regard to the Four P's.

Perspective

As they discussed their hopes for their community, Morehead residents tended to compare it, sometimes a bit enviously, to Mount Sterling, Ky., a community that is a couple of counties closer to the metropolitan hub of Lexington.

So NewCities staff set about holding up a mirror to Morehead residents to show them their advantages — not only compared to Mount Sterling, but to other benchmark communities.

For one thing, Morehead, unlike Mount Sterling, is home to a state university, which is a huge resource for any city. However, taking advantage of that resource had always been, well, complicated. Occasional partnerships between the university and the community never quite bridged the town/gown divide. Often local government officials wished aloud that the university would show more interest in the surrounding community, and the university wished the same in reverse.

However, if Morehead was to attract more and better jobs, Morehead State's involvement would be essential. Some tie-ins were obvious: Morehead State had recently become the location of a NASA satellite tracking antenna. Not only would the antenna be used to train a new generation of space scientists and engineers, but it could lead to business opportunities through the development of related patents.

True, the mirror also showed that Mount Sterling has its own advantages, including a higher per capita income, a flourishing industrial park and, yes, an Applebee's chain restaurant. But Morehead was also able to see that its per capita income had grown much faster in the last decade — and faster than other benchmark communities in Kentucky and other states.

And what about Morehead's place in the wider world? Plotted on a national map, Morehead is smack in the middle of three emerging "super cities" that are among eight identified by researchers at the University of Pennsylvania. The researchers estimate that nearly three-fourths of the U.S. population will live in or near all eight of these "super cities" by the year 2050.

That said, more than five million people live within 150 miles of downtown Morehead, including four metropolitan areas.

All this means that Morehead is well situated to attract workers and tourists, as well as to have access to the amenities — including the economic resources — of bigger cities and regions. At the same time, NewCities pointed out, Morehead is close enough to attract people seeking a different quality of life outside the big cities.

Place

Collins was surprised that, even as citizens talked eagerly about bringing new technology jobs to town, they insisted on preserving their local heritage. "Heritage matters more to people than I thought it did," he said. "Even people I thought would not be very interested in it are very interested in protecting our heritage as we move forward."

Citizens said they valued Morehead's small town charm, friendliness, attractive surroundings, education, arts and culture, health care, belief in local people and optimism.

They felt safe in their homes in spite of an escalating crime problem. And they believe they live in one of the most beautiful places in Kentucky with its national forest and Cave Run Lake.

When they talked about what they loved about their city, citizens repeatedly mentioned the downtown area. So, NewCities suggested, why not pull it all together? There would be no way to return Morehead's downtown to a nostalgic mix of A&P groceries and Western Auto stores, but it might include "cool shops" featuring trail gear, Appalachian crafts, local restaurants and weekend festivals. The community could advertise its Main Street as the place tourists must stop before they take off on trails in the forest or return home from boating at the lake.

People

In the same way the Morehead community tended not to think out of the box about Morehead State and how it could contribute to economic development, it was also missing opportunities presented by another university resource — all those kids. MSU had a reputation as a "suitcase school" where students go home on the weekend. The community admitted to something of a defeatist attitude about keeping young people in town. Morehead would never be able to provide music clubs and other hot spots — not to mention jobs after graduation — that are available in larger cities.

But given that Morehead students would be the doctors, research scientists and business gurus of tomorrow, why not plug into their desire to learn as part of Morehead's community-building efforts? Not only would it help the community today, but it would build connections between the town and the students that could encourage more of them to work and raise their families in Morehead after graduation.

As it turned out, a listening session with MSU students during the NewCities project helped to convince city leaders that there *were* both small and large steps they could take to engage them, including a bus stop on campus and an all-night restaurant.

Community leaders also began exploring the possibility of drawing students downtown as part of their studies. "The university is about one block from downtown. In some cities like this, you can't tell where the university ends and the city begins, but in Morehead, there are few students downtown," Collins said. "Already the Kentucky Center for Traditional Music at MSU holds classes downtown, and the center wants to expand into a larger downtown venue with their own concert hall. Not only would that help revitalize Main Street, but it would draw more students there and help preserve the local heritage," Collins explained. "That's two or three of our things under one."

NewCities suggested that the community and university also collaborate on similar Main Street programs — maybe even a restaurant where students could learn culinary and marketing skills while supporting Morehead's tourist industry.

Regardless of the specific initiatives, the community has also made an effort to ensure that students have a way to be heard in the community. The chamber of commerce, the city council and the NewCity Morehead Committee now have ex-officio student members.

Brian Gay, president of the MSU Student Body, helped bring that about. After he was first asked to serve as an ex-officio member of the chamber of commerce, Gay overheard someone with the chamber remark that a student representative wasn't the same as a regular ex-officio member — such as the university representative — because they were just going to change every year. "I was like, 'Dang,'" he said. But before he had to speak up, another member said that they still offered a valuable perspective from the student body. "I was really glad to hear someone else respond that way, other than myself," he said.

Prosperity

If economic development today is really about quality of life, citizens agreed that Morehead has a head start. It has one of the top public school districts in Kentucky, a community college satellite campus and a regional university; they could collaborate on dual-credit programs that would help local residents go to college, thus raising the community's level of education. The community might also develop property between downtown and the university to attract retirees who could enjoy MSU's intellectual amenities and be within walking distance of downtown. Pushing ahead with a planned family activities center for the region plus bike paths and more attractive green space would further enhance Morehead's quality of life and thus its economic prospects.

Citizens also realized that, if the community is to move forward in significant ways, they need to make hard decisions about the way local government is run — including whether to merge the city and county governments and change zoning rules. NewCities suggested that, rather than walk into a buzzsaw of opposition to either merger or zoning, the community work incrementally toward collaboration on city and county services and regulating local development.

But will Morehead be able to keep the good will and momentum going? The community now has a strong NewCity board and working committees made up of stakeholders from all facets of the community. The board, which includes only four elected officials, has been meeting monthly in order to work on Morehead's short-, medium- and long-term strategies.

Mayor Collins said he has already seen better cohesion among government agencies. According to Rodney Hitch with the local economic development council, "It is very exciting to see the leaders of the community and citizens alike come together for the common good."

The community decided it should try to make progress as soon as possible on short-term goals such as convincing the owner of a messy lot at the entrance of town to clean it up. City officials had worked on him for years; the difference this time, Collins said, was that he "knew the whole community was behind it." Morehead is putting up a new welcome sign there as well as another entrance into town with run-down buildings. And community leaders are developing signs for traffic lights so people can find their way around more easily. They are also collaborating with the medical center and MSU to support a new $28 million health facility and research center and starting a housing project for seniors and the handicapped.

Board members and elected officials also realize that sustainable community building involves ongoing dialogue among citizens, not just offering a few suggestions that others will implement.

And that issue — getting input from all members of the community — remains a challenge.

"How do we go forward to see that people have jobs and a reasonable standard of living — where they can have food in their bellies, a roof over their heads and take care of their health problems — and do that while protecting the environment and the natural beauty and the cultural heritage?" Professor Herron asks. "We've got to continue to tap that sentiment in the community and make sure that their interest and concerns are being addressed.

"I think to some extent it happened. I think it happened as well as I've ever seen it happen. But it's not over. That's got to continue. You have to be vigilant to make sure you provide sufficient opportunity for that to happen," Herron said.

"There is nothing more important, nothing more noble that you can do than to provide a family with a safe, decent affordable home."

Mayor Bradley Collins

One stock feature of political speeches is the homey story about a candidate's humble beginnings. The speaker often concludes by noting: "We didn't even know we were poor because no one else had much either."

That was *not* Morehead Mayor Bradley Collins' experience. Make no mistake about it; he knew his family had it rough.

He and his siblings sometimes slept four-to-a-bed in a small substandard home in West Morehead, Ky., a neighborhood blighted by crime, (barely) supported by welfare and crowded with misery. Basic needs, like indoor plumbing and insulation, were missing. The only good thing about sleeping four-to-a-bed was that in mid-winter it kept him warm. His mom washed all those children's clothes outside with a washboard.

"The housing was atrocious," he said. "We lived in terrible conditions…You couldn't invite a friend to come in because you'd be embarrassed."

It was almost too much for a child in that circumstance to dare to dream of having influence and power some day. But in America kids are allowed to dream big.

"I always thought if I ever could get out of there and get into a position where I could help, that was something I would love to do," he said, "because nobody deserves to grow up in those kinds of conditions."

Now serving his fourth term as the mayor of Morehead, Collins said his "main passion" is affordable housing. And in the last 14 years more than 80 houses have been built in West Morehead with the help of federal and regional grants and the assistance of other organizations. The new homes represent about four-fifths of the neighborhood.

For a place that didn't even have paved roads in his childhood it has been an astonishing turnaround, Collins said. Last year, he had the privilege to drive his sister, who had moved to Indiana, through the old neighborhood she hadn't seen in 30 years.

"She just cried like a baby," he said. "She said 'I can't believe you all did this.' "

Collins himself likes to drive through his old neighborhood at least once a week.

"If I could be proud of anything, it would be our housing program," he said. "There is nothing more important, nothing more noble that you can do than to provide a family with a safe, decent affordable home — a house to live in, a house they can pay for and call their own," he said. "It just does something for a family. It does something for their self-respect, for their self-esteem. It makes them a better family. It makes them better people. It makes them better partners for the community."

In addition to improving the lives of the families directly, it is also good for the community as a whole, Collins said, because it increases the tax base. He's now working on a plan to build a $7 million three-story apartment building for seniors and handicapped residents.

How did Collins make it all the way from West Morehead to the mayor's office?

He said his active engagement in civic affairs came almost by accident. His brother-in-law, a police officer, was concerned about some conflict between the mayor and city council. He asked Collins, who by then had experience in construction and insurance, to run for city council.

"He had to convince me," Collins said. "I never dreamed I would go into politics or government. But he said, 'We need people who will stand up for what is right, and we need people who won't go along with the status quo.' I still had to think about it. But I had always enjoyed watching government and listening to government and politics."

He ran and won. "I got hooked," he said. After a couple of terms on the council, he ran for an unexpired term as mayor and has been in the office ever since. "It's been quite an exciting road."

Not that it's always easy.

"It is very stressful and very aggravating. I usually think about resigning twice a week at least," he said with a laugh. "But it's very, very rewarding."

Brad is not kidding about the toll that has been taken on him in his role as mayor. Deeply religious and humble in the tradition of servant leadership, Brad is conflicted about decisions every day. He has broken ties on votes of the Morehead City Council that have cost him friendships and caused him to be shunned by some people in his hometown.

But he always tells me he has felt he had to do the right thing for the good of the whole community.

"When the window is open, you need to go through it."
Brian Gay

Brian N. Gay initially applied to Morehead State University as a "backup" school. There were other places he liked better, but MSU's location in Morehead, Ky., did fit his geographic criteria — to be about a two-hour drive from his parents' home in suburban Cincinnati, Ohio.

But when he actually toured MSU, he was blown away. "That's one of the things Morehead is really good at — bringing people in," he said. When he got to the admissions office, he was greeted by a sign that welcomed him by name. Compared to the cattle-herd experience at some other schools, the tour of the MSU campus involved just one other family.

And when decision time came, he chose Morehead — even though he also got accepted by his first-choice schools. He was taken with the "small town feel" and the personal attention. "I just decided right away this was the place for me," he said.

But during his freshman year some of the other realities of a small town experience began to sink in. Growing up in suburban Cincinnati, he had come to take for granted that he could find the services or products he needed easily. But suddenly he was in a place where restaurants were often closed on Sunday — certainly closed overnight — and "if Wal-Mart doesn't have it, you're screwed."

He also noticed that the student body didn't have the same sense of cohesion, or school spirit, that he was used to. He had graduated from Wyoming High School, which *Newsweek* magazine once named as one of the top 10 in the nation. There was a strong sense of school spirit there, he said. And everyone supported the sports teams.

In high school, "I didn't feel the need to step up because I felt satisfied with the way of life." But at MSU, he did feel the need to step up.

He first got involved at the dorm council level. He ran for president of his residence hall, the 14-floor Mignon Tower, and was elected. In that role he did many things he was proud of, such as helping organize a haunted house that took up all 14 floors. Not only did the event offer entertainment to the whole Morehead campus, but it also raised money and served to unite the dorm and get "neighbors" talking to each other.

By the end of his sophomore year he was interested in the Student Government Association. During his junior year he chaired the SGA's public relations committee and got involved in an effort to expand university meal plans. That didn't work out, but during the process student government leaders got to know Morehead chamber of commerce leaders.

As a senior Gay served as SGA vice president for public relations, which brought him attention as one of the "faces" of student government. He decided to run for SGA president at the end of his senior year, which was an option because he was staying on to work on a master's degree in public administration. He was elected and the day after he was sworn in, the chamber of commerce invited him to join as an ex-officio voting member.

The Morehead City Council followed suit by asking for a member of SGA to serve as a liaison — a role that another student had to fill because it conflicted with Gay's class schedule.

Around this same time the university's vice president of student life asked Gay and another SGA officer to go to city hall and talk to people working on the NewCities effort in Morehead. Basically, Gay said with a laugh, "they asked us to speak on behalf of all students."

Instead, he encouraged the organizers to invite students to discuss their feelings about the city openly at a "listening session" on campus. "I was all about jumping at that opportunity and trying to provide as much student input as possible," Gay said. "Because when the window is open, you need to go through it."

More than 75 students attended the meeting, called "Modernize Morehead," to talk about what they needed. "A lot of it was entertainment," Gay said. They wanted things to do downtown that they could walk to.

Gay believes the session had an impact: a 24-hour restaurant recently opened in Morehead, as did a Buffalo

Wild Wings restaurant. Morehead Mayor Brad Collins announced that the local transit agency would extend a bus line to serve the university. The bus system was designed for areas of town with older residents who needed to go shopping, Gay said. But students pointed out that they needed transportation to the same places.

"It is just pretty much a matter of putting a bench out there with a sign that said we're stopping here. They may have had to go a block out of their way," Gay said. But it probably wouldn't have happened before, because few if any students were communicating this need to city leaders.

Gay has also worked on the student body culture at Morehead. The school has had better attendance at athletic events in part because of scheduled bonfires and pep rallies to boost school spirit, he said. As he started his second term of office for the 2007-2008 school year, he was also looking forward to the first fall formal that the school would hold since the 1970s.

Gay says that it's hard sometimes for college students to see the payoff in investing in a place where they may only live for four years. (He had to personally try to explain this to many, many students who complained to him when the SGA recommended a $35 activity fee increase to fund a student recreation center that would probably not be completed for years.) That sort of delayed gratification is hard for any citizen, but may be especially hard for college students who do not expect to be around long-term.

"The projects that you work on, you may not see happen yourself," he said. "But the next person down the line is going to see the fruits of your labor."

He confessed there were times that even he considered moving on. "I can't tell you how many incomplete applications I had to other schools," he said. "I would just get frustrated." And he would think that his friends who touted the big-school advantages of a place like Ohio State were right.

But then, he'd have one of those good experiences and he would say: "I really love this place and I can't believe I was thinking about leaving...There is something about this place that just keeps bringing me back."

Ultimately Gay became an intern with the NewCities Institute and is working at Morehead State University to develop a NewCities "scorecard" for citizen engagement efforts.

As for the work of engaging people, Gay said he now knows first hand that it sometimes takes discontent to motivate them. A recent rule change at the university involving discounts given to out-of-state residents generated a lot of outrage and people went to the SGA to advocate for them. Whenever you have a large group of students "fired up," Gay said, "it is sort of, in my mind, a recruiting event for student involvement. If they get involved once, they may get hooked."

Regardless of where his career leads him, Gay said, he knows that he'll want to participate in community life. Should he get further education at another university, "the first thing I'd do is find their student government," he said. "And when I start my career I plan to seek out ways to engage myself in community development and the operation of local government."

~~~

Brian is a true community patriot – a college student making a difference in a city that has become his second home, and doing so because he feels the need to be involved. Brian also became a NewCities intern after working with us in Morehead, and will be helping activate the student government in another city where we are working with citizens and civic leaders. The best news is he's seriously considering a career in public service!

"The important consideration is not whether you contribute to society without being paid, but that what you do is contributing to society."

Dudley Herron

When J. Dudley Herron arrived on the campus of Purdue University as a newly-hired assistant professor, he quickly noted some basic facts of academic life. The road to tenure involved long hours, and most faculty members could be found in their laboratories on the weekend.

"I felt a strong commitment to my profession," he said. "But my three children were eight, six and one at the time, and I had a prior commitment to my wife and to them."

He'd work 60-hour weeks or more, he said. But he'd be home — or at the very least umpiring little league games — on the weekend. "My role as a father and husband would trump my role as chemical educator on occasion."

That was 1965. Despite taking all those weekends off he did make tenure and went on to have a satisfying and distinguished career.

But he also raised children and participated in community life — albeit mostly through church and youth activities. He judged speech meets, worked sports concession stands and chaperoned youth mission trips.

There were other relatively small projects — helping needy families at Christmas, for example. He also occasionally worked with Habitat for Humanity. "But my schedule was such that I just didn't have a lot of free time," he said. "Much of our contribution was financial. I didn't have time until I retired."

Retirement came in 1996. By then, Herron was back in his home state of Kentucky, where he had moved to chair the department of physical sciences at Morehead State University. He thought that retirement would give him a chance to get involved in his first love: science education in the public schools. (He had started his career as a high school science teacher in the days when Sputnik had made science classrooms a frontline during the Cold War.)

But the following spring he was diverted by another project. Jimmy Carter was coming to Kentucky for a "Hammering in the Hills" blitz. In one week Habitat for Humanity would build 50 homes, six of them in Morehead. The Morehead chapter needed a professional organizer, someone who could coordinate every detail from the former president's communication needs to the housing and feeding of 500 out-of-town volunteers.

Herron took on that role as a temporary, part-time executive director. As a result, he met people from outside the university circles he normally moved in. And new types of community issues began to interest him. "I've often said I don't have direction in life," he said. "I have always fallen into everything that I've done."

At that point, Herron took the next step toward getting involved in "the messiness of democracy." He served on a seemingly endless list of boards including the Morehead Sister Cities board, the local planning commission, the zoning adjustment board, the downtown revitalization board, a committee charged with updating the community development plan and the NewCity Morehead committee.

So what was it that has pulled Herron, personally, into community work? Certainly, as a retiree, he has the time for it now. But it also comes down to how he was brought up: Herron was raised in a community where people needed to work together for the common good.

"I just like to be useful," he said. He was raised mostly by his mother's parents in the tiny town of Kevil, in western Kentucky. For a family to survive in that time and place they had to rely on the help of neighbors. Kevil had a lot of strawberry farms then, and when the harvest was in, everyone worked together — picking their own strawberries and then helping their neighbors.

"We didn't have much. In that time, *nobody* had much, certainly not compared to the kind of things my children think are necessities," Herron said with a laugh. "My grandmother made all her clothes. My grandfather built the house we lived in... It was a small community where helping one another was part of life."

His grandmother would sit with the sick and the homebound. His grandfather, an electrician from the coal mines, helped wire the neighbor's homes for electricity when it first came to the region.

Herron's own adult life was, of course, very different. But community involvement can take many forms.

"Like most married couples with limited re-sources, our early years were primarily devoted to survival," he said. He and his wife, Joyce, were active in church, but early on, when he was a public school teacher and she was a nurse, they didn't see community involvement as something "extra" they needed to do. "We saw our jobs as places of service and had little time for volunteer activities that weren't work related."

Herron said, "The important consideration is not whether you contribute to society without being paid but that what you do is contributing to society." He added, "Is the chemical engineer making $200,000 a year and volunteering for Habitat for Humanity 20 hours a week contributing any more than the high school chemistry teacher or staff nurse making $30,000 a year and never volunteering because all of their free time is devoted to his or her students or patients and their problems?"

~~~

Dudley was the guy with the stick behind the scenes throughout the NewCities work in Morehead. I don't mean that he forced people to stay in line; rather, he encouraged and even nudged people forward when needed, and he stood in the way of retreat. One key trait of a community patriot is the willingness to take a chance on change. Dudley took the chance — and made a difference along the way.

CHAPTER EIGHT

ANOTHER CITY ACTING INTENTIONALLY: SPARKS, NEVADA

Sparks, Nev., was not one of the pilot communities for NewCities, but we learned a lot while working with citizens and city leaders as they sought ways to encourage more meaningful citizen participation. Here's the story.

~~~

You've undoubtedly heard of Reno, Nev., but perhaps not of Sparks, a smaller city only eight miles away in the same county. Thus the question comes up often: Is Sparks a town unto itself, or a bedroom community of the well-known gaming and entertainment capital?

City leaders decided long ago that Sparks should maintain its identity, separate from its celebrity neighbor. Sparks has consistently opposed merging government services with Reno. It has adjusted the rules for developers to limit sprawl. It has revitalized the downtown area, including the addition of condominiums and town homes.

It has even rewritten the city's mission statement to emphasize its small town atmosphere. The mission says Sparks will focus on "maintaining and enhancing the quality of life, fulfilling employment, recreational and educational opportunities for all, and by utilizing neighborhoods as the building blocks of the City of Sparks."

However, Sparks must also deal with the reality of being a fast-growing community in the fastest-growing state in America. Northern Nevada, where Reno and Sparks are located, is attractive because of its temperate climate. Reno and Sparks are adjacent to Lake Tahoe and a short drive to the California capital of Sacramento; Las Vegas is about eight hours southeast.

The Reno-Sparks area has been growing exponentially for years, and growth exploded during the recent housing boom. In 2005 alone the sales volume of homes in Reno and Sparks increased 27 percent, according to the *Nevada Business Journal,* and the average home price rose 20 percent to more than $400,000. Sparks now has three casinos and will soon have a fourth.

Learning about citizen participation

For civic leaders, managing this rate of growth must be a bit like riding a bucking bronco, and the city has periodically sought out citizen input on growth decisions. For instance, when Sparks got the chance to build a lake and marina, the city held local meetings to find out what amenities citizens wanted. More recently, the city did a professional survey to find out if citizens wanted casinos in their neighborhoods, which they did not.

"It's always been a community-oriented town," said Linda Patterson, executive administrator in the city manager's office.

But until recently, the city wasn't actively focusing on improving citizen engagement with the goal in mind of actually getting some hands-on help with the community's challenges.

The city got a wake-up call in 2003 when it lost its bid to be designated as an "All-America City" by the National Civic League, which cited lack of citizen participation as one of the reasons.

But more importantly city leaders began to realize that their community had some even harder decisions to make. All that growth during the housing boom was putting pressure on city services, and council members were anticipating a public debate in the near future over the need to raise taxes or generate more tax revenue. Nevada cities depend on the state sales tax and property tax, and the council wanted to consider its options. If Sparks was to push for changes, however, its citizens would have to understand the alternatives and the trade-offs involved.

The effort it takes

Elected officials also realized that the tax issue would come and go, but other issues would take its place. Thus they were ready to invest in citizen participation. Sparks City

Councilmember Ron Schmitt, also a member of the National League of Cities Advisory Council, became aware of the work of the NewCities Institute and played an instrumental role in bringing its ideas to Sparks.

Patterson, in the city manager's office, helped organize a leadership summit with NewCities in October 2006 to launch an initiative called Sparks Municipal Initiatives and Leadership Effort (SMILE). The summit brought together 36 council members, civic leaders and regular citizens — all referred to as "community champions" — to volunteer for citizen committees that would begin identifying and impacting local priorities.

The priorities developed by the citizens and elected officials included six areas: youth, diversity and inclusiveness; encouraging a healthier city; honoring history, art and tradition; balancing growth and quality of life; citizen involvement and leadership; and building business and community partnerships.

It was five months later, however, before the committees began working. Shortly beforehand, Sparks hired Marc De La Torre to organize the SMILE program as the citizen services coordinator for the city. And after all that time, "one of those challenges was bringing those citizens back," De La Torre said. Some had moved away; others seemed to have fallen off the face of the earth.

So he and the city's public information officer, Adam Mayberry, made a plan to "reintroduce" SMILE to the public. They mailed out SMILE inserts in the water bills, wrote op-eds in the local newspaper and chamber of commerce newsletter and featured SMILE on the government access television channel and the city website.

De La Torre also spoke to civic groups such as Kiwanis, Sertoma and Rotary and did an interview on the radio. And he put the word out the old-fashioned way: "I asked our current SMILE members to recruit friends and neighbors."

The committees were reconstituted and their work began.

However, it was immediately clear there was another challenge to deal with.

The citizen members of the committees often didn't have any idea what the city was already doing in the priority areas. "They thought there was this big vacuum out here," but a lot is already happening, Patterson said.

Frustrating as that was for city council members, who were helping lead the committees, it was an important lesson for them, Patterson said. "They needed to understand that the citizens' lives don't revolve around the city government."

Patterson and De La Torre prepared an inventory of what was already going on in the city, and De La Torre arranged for city department heads to help educate the committees about city projects.

After gaining that perspective on their community, some of the citizens began seeing possibilities. The youth and diversity group, for instance, "suggested we start the very first Sparks Youth City Council," De La Torre said.

"Their passion was to reach out to youth and make them feel their voice was important to the city. Citizens will recruit students and organize the youth council's structure to make it relevant to youth issues in the city and issues before our council. Our hope is that our local school district will give school credit for this activity." The next step was for all the committees to begin translating suggestions into action, De La Torre said. His role was to facilitate and to strike a balance between encouraging innovation and offering the occasional reality check.

"I do encourage out of the box thinking. In government we become so structured in thinking one way for a solution it can be refreshing to have someone from the outside give another perspective," he said.

De La Torre is also intent on helping citizens look for solutions rather than spend their committee time fuming about problems in the community. "Complaints are fine for a short period because it does bring issues to the table," he said. "However, SMILE's main purpose is to explore how our citizens can work with our elected officials and staff to bring about solutions."

ANOTHER CITY ACTING INTENTIONALLY: SPARKS, NEVADA

"They decided to close it down. The next thing I knew, I was picking it up and rebuilding it."

Linda Patterson

Linda and Bill Patterson moved to Sparks, Nev., in 1993. Bill was retired, and they weren't happy in Oregon — they found the winters too cold and the politics too liberal. They had always enjoyed visiting the Reno area, and they decided to relocate there.

Linda, who had been a district sales manager for Avon, looked for a different kind of job with regular hours and good benefits. She was soon hired by the City of Sparks as a police assistant taking crime reports.

But the drive and independence that had made her successful at the cosmetics giant helped her work her way up quickly. Today she is executive administrator in the city manager's office.

She has assisted on projects to encourage citizen participation. She organizes annual public attitude surveys, serves as project leader for the customer service team and helps coordinate leadership summits and various retreats and forums. She is also the editor of the Sparks monthly citizen e-newsletter.

Her dedication to her community, however, has carried over into other projects.

A few years ago she was recruited to join the board of the local homeless shelter, operated by Faith House Ministries, which served women with drug and alcohol problems. Board members were seeking her administrative skills.

However, Patterson wasn't content to just skim the surface. She became concerned when she realized the shelter itself had some physical problems: for one thing, it was located in an old house with some serious safety hazards, including a 100-year-old oil furnace. The board found the problems overwhelming.

"They decided to close it down. The next thing I knew, I was picking it up and rebuilding it," she said.

This was almost literally true — Patterson was on her own. At the same time, Patterson, who has a strong faith, believed that God was working through her. She was determined to refurbish the old home, which needed everything from a roof to a new foundation, and again provide transitional housing for women.

As director of women's ministries in her church, Patterson was interested in the struggles of women in crisis who couldn't get on their feet, especially in such an affluent community. Suppose they got behind on their rent and were evicted, she said. How could they ever get another place — which requires paying a deposit plus the first and last month's rent — when they were likely earning only $9 or $10 per hour? Inevitably, many became homeless. "I just couldn't let that continue," she said.

Patterson's idea was to give women a place to stay for six months to save money and gain skills: the shelter would no longer treat active addicts because of the costs of clinical treatment. Perhaps they wanted to get an apartment, or find a better job, or even regain custody of their children.

So in 2006 she and a few others formed a nonprofit called the Hosanna Home to replace the previous shelter; a proposal was submitted to Faith House Ministries and they donated the old house and monies from the sale of another Faith House Ministries property.

The house essentially had to be rebuilt from the ground up. During the past year at least six churches have contributed to the project, along with area businesses and dozens of volunteers. The Hosanna Home organizers have also trained 65 volunteers to train and coach the women in a variety of areas including life skills and careers.

"Today, Hosanna Home is the only transitional shelter for women in the Reno-Sparks area," Patterson said. In 2007 she received a "Making a Difference for Women" award from the Soroptimists, a service organization for business and professional women who help women in their local community.

"Linda is one of the most compassionate women I have been associated with," said her boss, Sparks City Manager Shaun Carey.

~~~

Linda is among those unsung public employees — and I've met many of them — whose passion for her community spills over in everything she does. She has gone beyond meeting the basic obligations of an employee and board member to embrace the opportunities for true citizenship that those roles provide.

CHAPTER NINE

MAKING A DIFFERENCE TOGETHER

One of my favorite movies, *Out of Africa,* is based on the life of Isak Dinesen, a Dane who spent most of her life in her beloved Africa as an entrepreneur and champion of the native population; among other things, she built a school for children.

At the end of the movie, following financial reverses and the death of someone dear, Dinesen looks at the morning sun rising over Mount Kilimanjaro. Will it "reflect a color that I have worn?" she wonders.

Her question is whether, with all her efforts, she really made a difference. This is true for all of us: As human beings, we have deep ties to place and a desire for lives of meaning and legacy. Those ties and that desire are at the heart of the NewCities message about citizens and community building.

Leadership is a quality that is as old as time yet it is sorely missing today — at least in the forms in which we once knew it. We are bewildered by a world grown wild and large beyond our control. We want instant answers just as we want instant coffee and instant news. We don't really connect in a hyper-connected universe.

But these are only superficial obstacles as we pursue what Isak Dinesen knew was fundamental to the human spirit — "to make the world a better place for those that follow."

Still, where do we begin?

At NewCities we begin with the fundamentals. Citizens have choices: to be intentional in our citizenship and to live in ways that have meaning, even when decisions are painful, or to retreat to our inner sanctuaries and hope that things turn out all right. Citizenship is not and never should be as easy as serving on boards or always taking the lead on a project. Sometimes leadership is about follow-ship. Sometimes it is about compromise. Sometimes it is about holding your ground.

Adlai Stevenson once observed that the fundamental strength of democracy lay in the willingness of the citizen to be conflicted every single day about the important decisions that must be made. Citizenship is about having different views – whether they're labeled conservative or liberal – but understanding the bigger picture that exists beyond one's own interests.

Our country is a great one that has nevertheless made many mistakes along the way. What is remarkable in our history, however, is the ability of the American people, one community at a time, to come together to work toward solutions. Ever optimistic, we aim for perfection but never achieve it. Yet therein lies the beauty of citizenship. Unlike

Google, which can provide immediate responses to your burning questions, democracy does not provide an instant answer. It just provides a process for getting better every day.

Of course there are those who say that at 200-plus years our democracy is fraying around the edges. They say no democracy has ever lasted so long.

I say we prove them wrong. We can take lessons from around the world. In a recent visit to Romania I was struck by the vigor and desire of the people for strong local communities and for democracy. They're eager to learn from Americans. Coming out of a dictatorship and revolution as well as decades of Soviet rule, their passion for democracy and participatory governance should put the United States to shame.

Earlier in the book I recalled a conversation I had with the mayor of Beirut, Lebanon, at a conference in Boston, Mass. He told me how he had spent a great deal of time in the U.S. and even in Kentucky. His enthusiasm was palpable as he described the restoration of his beautiful city following the assassination of former prime minister Rafik Hariri and the previous bombings and riots.

The downtown, he observed, was coming back. His description of one business sprouting up and then another made me think of a neglected garden that, in spite of all else, returns to health. There is something about the human spirit that is like that garden, resilient and fruitful in the face of overwhelming obstacles.

It was shortly after that conference that the latest war broke out and the city was once again destroyed. I think often of that mayor and how it is my belief that his optimism lives on and that his city will grow back. And I think then about how much we in this country take for granted.

All this boils down to our vigilance and strength. Are we willing to do what needs to be done to make our country great, one community at a time? As my father observed, we must take a bit of the old and traditional and a bit of the new and use it all to our advantage. One of the best stories about this comes from Vaughn Grisham, director of The McLean Institute for Economic Development in Oxford, Miss.

"My main story," he told the Saguaro Seminar on Civic Engagement in America at Harvard, "is about a small town's need to buy a big stud bull." Grisham recounted how George McLean, a progressive newspaper owner, helped turn Tupelo, Miss., into a leading dairy county in the 1940s by convincing business owners to, yes, invest in the bull. Along the way, McLean pointed out to a skeptical hardware store owner that he'd never earn more than $6,000 a year if his customers couldn't earn more than $600.

"McLean believed that our social fabric and our economic fabric are pretty tightly interwoven," Grisham said. "If we care enough to look for it, we can always find a thread that binds us. And, if you look at it, to say that we have an obligation to help each other out is actually a traditional American, and very pragmatic, point of view."

It is after all true that the qualities of leadership have not changed. It has always chafed against conventional thinking, going back even further in history to Sojourner Truth. Once she was speaking to a group when a man in the audience shouted up to her, "I don't care anymore for you than I would a tiny little flea!"

"Well," she replied, "then it is my job to make you itch even more."

Her work and the work of great humanitarians such as Martin Luther King, Jr. — which seems so obvious and necessary today — was to free an entire people. Our work is to save our communities one at a time...and perhaps, paradoxically, to save the world.

Leaving our comfort zones will allow us to learn about what makes a great community. By opening our minds to the possibilities we can overcome the apathy that is sending us into our houses at night only to shut out the world.

Finally and perhaps most importantly, we must overcome the arrogance of believing not only that our way is the only way, but that we are doing enough. If we can envision more, we can accomplish it.

I grew up close to the park that commemorates Orville and Wilbur Wright and their famous first flight. For the longest time as a child I actually believed they flew off that ledge that overlooks the highway!

But the Wright brothers had a dream — and look how it changed the world. That ingenuity sprung from good old sturdy Dayton, Ohio, and the same ingenuity is waiting to flower in communities all over America and the world. We as citizens can see the possible for the places we love. And we can become the everyday heroes, the community patriots, who make it happen.

I know it can be done because I've seen it, and it must be done for the future of our towns and cities. We need our everyday heroes, our community patriots, to help us move with confidence throughout the 21st century.

THE NEWCITIES INSTITUTE

WHO WE ARE

Citizenship - in a word, it is what the NewCities Institute is all about. The NewCities Institute, dedicated to developing civic capacity in communities, has identified 12 timeless principles that will help communities build economic and social prosperity by and through citizen engagement. We see communities as the sum of four components: people, place, perspective, and prosperity.

We believe that citizen involvement is a lifelong journey and should be as much a part of our daily routine as going to work and raising a family. We are committed to helping people where they live – in the trenches, on the ground, in communities – to improve their quality of life and grow to their full potential.

OUR MISSION

The mission of the NewCities Institute is to define and promote the economic and social prosperity of communities, regardless of size or location, through citizen engagement.

Visit www.newcities.org to learn more about Sylvia L. Lovely and the work of the NewCities Institute.

THE TWELVE PRINCIPLES OF
COMMUNITY BUILDING

PERSPECTIVE

Feed the Mind, Nurture the Soul — Cities must be committed to a life-long learning process, devoted to a better quality of life.

Connect to the World — Connections to the greater world are critical. Communities must be able to use and benefit from them through training and receptivity to innovation, technologies and ideas.

Buy Locally, Sell Globally — Keeping money in the local community allows the money to multiply, promoting loyalty to the community, charitable giving, and political involvement.

PLACE

Remain True to the City's Uniqueness — Though cities may share many similarities with other cities, each is distinct from all others. To succeed, cities must build on who they are and what they have.

Don't Merely Grow, Plan and Develop Over Time — The primary focus of development is and should be increasing quality, not quantity.

Build Beautifully and Steward the Environment — Managing the building process along with natural resources of the environment create a high quality of life, attracting people and businesses who create jobs and income.

LEADERSHIP

Cultivate Leadership and Citizen Involvement — The citizen leadership and involvement must be cultivated and embraced.

Encourage Youth, Diversity, and Inclusiveness — If a community collectively recognizes youth, diversity and inclusiveness as an important part of its fabric, then the individuals in that community are better prepared to deal with the larger world.

Embrace Healthy Living — Cities that encourage infrastructure and programs for a healthy lifestyle improve the quality of life in a community and allow its citizens to reap the health benefits and economic advantages afforded to a more active way of life.

PROSPERITY

Recruit, Retain, and Generate Wealth — Cities must work to attract new businesses and new residents, while nurturing existing ones.

Mimic Bigness, but Think Small — Imitation is the truest form of flattery. Successful projects in larger cities can often be replicated on a smaller scale in smaller cities.

Rethink Boundaries — Cities should work with surrounding counties and local governments to see that needed services are provided effectively and efficiently.

NewCities in America Series

■ This Little Blue Book details how people can get involved in their communities and gives examples of cities and individuals already getting big results. Valuable for everyday citizens and elected officials alike, it will help people gain a spirit of mission and commitment to action that can transform their communities.

■ Sylvia L. Lovely
■ 128 pages
■ Paperback $14.95
■ ISBN: 0-9760713-0-4

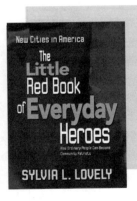

■ Sylvia L. Lovely
■ Published by The Clark Group, Lexington, Ky.
■ 176 pages, includes 16 pages of color photographs
■ Paperback $19.95
■ ISBN: 978-1-883589-85-1

Quantity Discounts Available
Call The Clark Group
800-944-3995
or order online at www.theclarkgroupinfo.com